THE
SUBCONSCIOUS
MIND
AND THE
CHALICE

TORKOM
SARAYDARIAN

Visions for the Twenty-First Century®

The Subconscious Mind and the Chalice

©1993 The Creative Trust

ISBN: 0-929874-18-8

Library of Congress Catalog Card Number: 91-92898

Printed in the United States of America

Cover Design: *Fine Point Graphics*
                       Sedona, Arizona

Printed by: *Data Repoductions Corp.*
                       Rochester Hills, Michigan

Published by: **T.S.G. Publishing Foundation, Inc.**
                       Visions for the 21st Century®
                       P.O. Box 4273
                       West Hills, California 91308
                       United States of America

Note: The visualizations and exercises contained in this book are given as guidelines. They should be used with discretion and after receiving professional advice.

Table of Contents

Diagrams

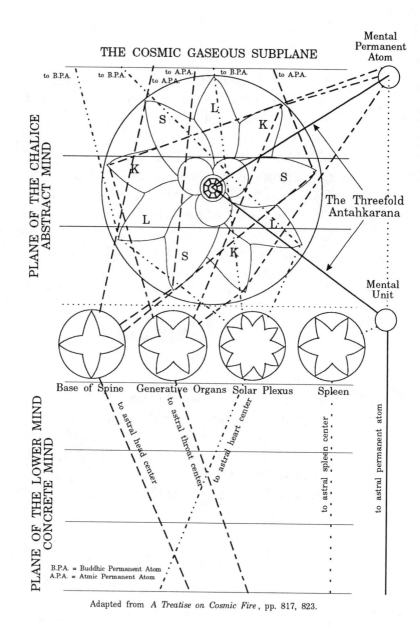

THE COSMIC GASEOUS SUBPLANE

Mental Permanent Atom

PLANE OF THE CHALICE ABSTRACT MIND

to B.P.A. to B.P.A. to A.P.A. to B.P.A. to A.P.A.
to A.P.A.

L
S
K
K
S
L
S
K

The Threefold Antahkarana

Mental Unit

Base of Spine   Generative Organs   Solar Plexus   Spleen

to astral head center
to astral throat center
to astral heart center
to astral spleen center
to astral permanent atom

PLANE OF THE LOWER MIND CONCRETE MIND

B.P.A. = Buddhic Permanent Atom
A.P.A. = Atmic Permanent Atom

Adapted from *A Treatise on Cosmic Fire*, pp. 817, 823.

Diagram 0-1 The Chalice

A Few Words

This book is composed of two sections. The first one is the subconscious mind. The second one is the Chalice. The study of the subconscious mind eventually leads us to the real Treasury within us which is the Chalice.

The subconscious mind is filled with all our automatic thoughts, speech, and actions. When we have no power over them, they often lead us into embarrassing situations. The study of the subconscious mind helps us control these automatic thoughts, speech, and actions.

The study of the Chalice helps us to discover the treasury of creative forces within our being and gradually learn how to use them for the advantage of humanity.

The Chalice is one of the parts of the human psychic mechanism built within the sphere of the human mind. It serves as a treasury for the human being at the time of his needs. It also provides him with vision and hope for the future.

Within this treasury is saved all that man thinks, speaks, and does in harmony with Beauty, Goodness, Righteousness, Joy, Freedom, striving toward perfection, and sacrificial service. All such thoughts, words, and actions are collected within this inner treasury as a savings for the future to be used in many lives to come.

The awareness of this fascinating subject opens new horizons in our consciousness and a new state of security, knowing that not even a cup of water is lost when given to a thirsty man.

In this treasury also are collected all the pearls of experiences and distilled wisdom of the ages.

Thus, the Chalice contains all the true knowledge, the real love, the pure sacrifices the person has accumulated throughout his many lifetimes. They collect in this repository, and, life after life, the person is filled with the results of his own virtues, his own beauty. The Chalice contains what is often called *Grace*, which floods a person in times of need. It is the contents of the Chalice that add the beauty and depth to our life and offer the most direct link to the inner creative Source and to Higher Worlds.

The subconscious mind is in the levels of the mental plane that are submerged below the threshold of our conscious mind. It is the repository of all disjointed experiences of pain, suffering, fear, confusion. These experiences can be mixed with joy or with sorrow.

The Path of the human soul is slowly to dissipate these subconscious elements and to clean out the barns of the subconscious mind. The Path of the human soul is to act, think, feel, and speak in the light of his Chalice. It is only when the subconscious elements are dissipated that a person is deemed a free man. Until then, his life is conditioned by the contents that surface automatically when a link is made to them.

The subconscious mind contains records of millions of years. It contains urges and drives, hypnotic suggestions, and commands which lead our life toward destruction.

In this storage we have also the recording of many happy moments interrupted by moments of suffering and pain.

One of the greatest healing processes will begin when we discover ways to free ourselves from our own subconscious mind. The first part of this book will tell you more about this fascinating story.

PART I

The
Subconscious Mind

1 | The Subconscious Mind

Various psychologists and related professionals use the term "subconscious mind" as something that has great power to transform human life or to grant wishes to human beings. However, the Ageless Wisdom uses the term "subconscious mind" to refer to a special mental "diskette" which records all that we think, imagine, dream, hear, smell, and feel while we are in a state of unconsciousness. The Chalice is just the opposite of the subconscious mind. The Chalice accumulates all that is experienced in the moments of clear consciousness, and only those elements that are related to Beauty, Goodness, Righteousness, Joy, Freedom, gratitude, solemnity, and other such qualities.

Some people think that the subconscious mind is a storage space where certain powers, virtues, great ideas, beauty, and wisdom are accumulated. In the Ageless Wisdom this is the Chalice, not the subconscious mind.

In the Chalice are found all the elements of true leadership, sacrificial labor, love, and wisdom. The Chalice is the source of all powers and energies that can transmute, transform, and transfigure the life of an individual or of humanity.

The Ageless Wisdom considers the subconscious mind as a depository of hindrances, pain and suffering, joy and horror chained together, and happiness and horror fused together.

Certain definitions will make things clearer for the reader.

The *conscious mind*, or concrete mind, refers to the fourth subplane of the mental plane.

The *subconsciousness* is located within the lower mental planes — levels seven, six, and five. Esoterically, these levels are called "levels under the Threshold," especially levels six and seven since level five is sometimes active.

The *Unconscious* refers to those states of consciousness which stand out of our conscious reach. For example, the states of consciousness or of awareness[1] found in the Spiritual Triad and in Monadic and Divine Planes are out of our reach. These states — and still higher states in planetary and solar consciousness — are for us states of Unconsciousness.

---

1.   See *The Science of Becoming Oneself*, Ch. 10.

When we move into the Spiritual Triad, intuitional and atmic awareness become a part of our awareness. And, when we build the higher Antahkarana, the Monadic and Divine Planes become part of our awareness...and so on.

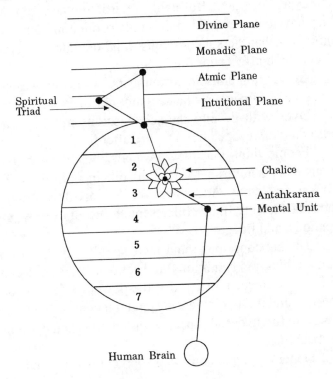

Diagram 1-1 The Mental Plane

The term the Unconsciousness in this book is not synonymous with the Superconsciousness. Levels three, two, and one of the mental plane are referred to as the *Superconsciousness.* If you are not conscious on those three levels, they are part of the Unconsciousness for you.

Also, beyond the mental plane, any plane is the Superconsciousness when you are aware of all that is going on there.

There was a time when the seventh, sixth, and fifth levels of the mind were levels where the human consciousness operated. But at this stage of human evolution, they have been left behind. It is only in our non-conscious moments that the subconscious mind operates, registers events, and affects our life.

In our non-conscious moments, whatever we feel, whatever we imagine, whatever thoughtforms we identify ourselves with go into the subconscious mind and accumulate there, age after age, life after life.

People think that they are conscious at every moment. This is not true. Most of the time people are 80% - 90% unconscious. And whenever they are unconscious, the subconscious mind collects thousands of events, suggestions, and images.

The subconscious mind increasingly has control of human thinking, conditions, and actions. The world conditions are in such a state that the power of the subconscious mind is daily increasing, and if it continues in such a way, in future decades people will totally act like robots or machines.

Generally, an unconscious moment is a moment

1. When you have passed out

2. When you are in pain

3. When you suffer

4. When you are worried

5. When you fall into anxiety

6. When you are in the grip of fear, anger, or hatred

7. When you do something against your conscience

8. When you slander and fall into treason

9. When you are insulted, defeated, have failed, or have been beaten down

10. When your rights are violated or taken away from you

11. When you are under pressure from other human beings

12. When you commit a crime

13. When you commit murder

14. When you are depressed

15. When you are hypnotized

16. When you are revengeful or intensely irritated

17. When you live in vanity

18. When you are touchy

19. When you experience ugliness

20. When you see horror

21. When you are under the influence of alcohol, drugs, or under anesthesia

22. When you are excited, hilarious, or "spacey"

The list can be greatly extended, but the important thing is to know that in such moments our subconscious mind is actively registering events and controlling our mechanisms.

The subconscious mind not only registers things while we are "awake" but also when we are asleep. In sleep we gather much trash in our subconscious mind and also release much trash through our incoherent dreams and hallucinations. Sometimes we meet with the same negative conditions in the astral plane as we had in the physical plane. During these moments we collect astral events in our subconscious mind. Certain frightening dreams or attacks from our enemies or dark forces go directly into the subconscious mind *IF* we are not "awake" on the astral plane.[2]

Some dark forces project very depleting, destructive images into our subconscious mind which eventually affect our life. Also, people are very happy to sit in front of the television and watch movies about high levels of crime, violence, ugliness, and horror. The entire movie sinks into the subconscious mind.

If, in the future, people seriously investigate the causes of crimes, they will see a close connection between movies and increase of crime. But the public is brainwashed, hypnotized, and rendered unconscious to such a degree by the violence, crime, murder, and horror that it has no drive to stand against it. You can see how the opposition against crime, violence, and ugliness is slowly

---

2. For further information on the astral plane and sleep, see *Other Worlds* and *New Dimensions in Healing*.

dying out. Movies of ugliness, crime, and violence are attracting the largest audiences.

2 | Accumulations of the Subconscious Mind

When the subconscious mind accumulates a suffi-
cient amount of events, it slowly blocks your conscious
mind, takes control, and rules your life. From that moment
on, you are a sleeping fool who lives and acts by push-
buttons.

Any associative event puts your subconscious mind
into action. Even if 10% of your consciousness is left, the
subconsciousness blocks that too and dominates your life.

It is frightening but true: great masses of people act
like herds once you push the right buttons in them. Certain
politicians and political interests are famous for knowing
what push-buttons to use to manipulate the masses for
their own interests. The irony is that almost all the people

who are acting under the domination of the subconscious mind are not aware of it but think they are normal, conscious people, consciously thinking and living in the world.

How can you make a breakthrough and realize that you are acting under your subconscious mind?

The first step is to learn how to observe your behavior, your thinking, your speech, and your actions. If this step is not successful, try the second step.

Find a person whom you trust, a person who is awake, and ask him to observe you and tell you the moment you stop being conscious and fall under the dominance of your subconscious mind. Family members are the best spiritual teachers who can point out the moment your subconscious mind is acting through you.

Subconscious influences appear in your actions and words that are contradictory to your principles or the principles toward which you strive. Sometimes even you yourself can notice contradictions between what you think, what you say, and what you do.

Most of the time your subconscious mind acts when you are in the presence of people with whom you have subconscious links. While you are acting normally with one person, a new person comes with whom you have subconscious ties, and immediately your behavior changes. You do not see such changes, but your husband, wife, teacher, or your friends may see it.

It is interesting to know that your consciousness can hide what you are, but the subconsciousness reveals what you are. People who know how to read the expressions of your subconscious mind can easily know what you are.

This is why you must have a truthful, awake, and alert friend or a teacher who will watch you and let you know when and how you acted under the subconscious mind.

Once your friends or teachers make you see the moments and character of your changes, you can start observing yourself and find the very interesting ways your subconscious mind acts or manifests.

The faithful friend observing you will reveal how at certain times you acted "weird," when you were real, when you were unreal, when you were cosmetic, when you were natural, when you were changing or coming under the influence of your subconscious elements, and when you were coming out of the dominance of your subconscious mind.

A third method to control the subconscious tides is analysis. Analysis is observation plus an effort to find the origin of events, their relationship, and their possible affects on others.

For example you noticed, or others pointed out, that when a particular lady enters a room full of people, you begin to rub your nose. This is observation. To find out why you are doing that is the process of analysis.

Through your analysis, you may get to the root of the problem and discover the causes behind that action. Once you find the causes, the subconscious recording has meaning, and everything that has meaning comes to the surface of the logical mind. After a subconscious event has surfaced, then the logical mind can dissolve it either immediately or gradually. The event may be fabricated or real; it does not matter. It dies like a fish when it is pulled out of the pool of the subconscious mind.

To live under the commands of the subconscious mind means to live in your past failures, defeats, pain, suffering, disappointments, hurt feelings, losses, and horrors. To live in the past means you are asleep. Individuals, groups, and nations that live in the past cannot develop a mind which can see clearly the present situation and live for the future.

Any time you realize that you cannot control whatever you are doing, know that you are under the power of your subconscious mind. If you cannot control your mouth, your gossip, your idle talk and cursing, it is your subconscious mind that is controlling you. Any time you cannot stop the thoughts that you want to stop, you are under the control of the subconscious mind. Any time that you cannot stop your actions or your habits of eating, drinking, doping, smoking, and your sexual drives and urges, your subconscious mind is ruling your life.

As your control increases over your thinking, talking, feeling, and acting, the power of your subconscious mind decreases and slowly vanishes.

When your subconscious mind controls your life, your consciousness cannot expand and develop. You cannot advance spiritually. You cannot see reality. You cannot see the true causes of events. You fail in the purpose of your life even if you have financial success. The subconscious mind sometimes helps you be successful by making you associate with people who are asleep. But eventually you awaken in disaster.

All those people who become rich for the sake of richness, or use their money to lead people into deeper sleep, eventually fall into disastrous calamities in their lives. For example, drug sellers, people who make money in the business of prostitution, or make money through treason, or achieve high positions through killing people sooner or later face disasters.

The subconscious mind raises you up, up to the sky so that when you fall down to earth, not a single bone in your body is left unbroken. The subconscious mind does not let you have permanent friends because you always change and always contradict yourself and fall into confusion.

The subconscious mind cannot create a stable family, cannot have good relations with children, especially when your family members fall under the dominance of their subconscious mind. It is in that moment when confusion reigns that pain, suffering, and hatred run free in the streets of your life. The subconscious mind makes you live the same miserable life that your parents lived. If they were fighting, drinking, doping, or living a poor life, you live like them in order to be comfortable. Your subconscious mind never fails to make you imitate your parents, to make you sick, unhappy, and depressed. Every time you make an effort to resist your subconscious mind, you feel you are losing yourself, so you turn back and follow its lead.

If your parents were poor and you collected many subconscious elements of poverty, anytime you have an opportunity to be rich, you back off and do things that lead you to poverty.

Most of the politicians in the world promise changes because promises are often related to the subconscious mind; but if they do not keep their promises, it means they were acting under their subconscious mind when they were making the promises.

When you are planning to change things, to make breakthroughs, but do not do them, it means your subconscious mind is preventing you from achieving your goals. Often you rationalize and fabricate the reasons why you were not able to be successful in actualizing your plans. The fact is that all these excuses were fabrications of your subconscious mind. Unless these fabrications are realized and removed, you will always find "reasonable" excuses for why you did not reach your goal.

The worldwide situation follows the same rule. Leaders plan and sign agreements. But when the subconscious mind in the nation or in the world rules, the plans and intentions of the leaders are diverted toward totally opposite directions. One day, when people learn how to clean the stables of the subconscious mind of individuals, they will start working to clean the subconscious mind of nations, especially of those nations whose subconscious mind is flooded with elements of superiority, violence, separatism, and fanaticism.

When the cleansing process starts, they will see that their age-long suffering and pain were caused by their own subconscious mind. The subconscious mind of nations fills itself with recordings, especially when the nation is pursuing violent actions against its minorities, neighbors, or even fomenting war or revolution.

A nation that uses fear and force to control its people is often destroyed by the eruption of the people's subconscious mind.

The United Nations came into being in a moment of true realization of a world vision. But what has happened since? The subconscious elements of nations slowly destroyed the activity of the United Nations by obeying the suggestions of the subconscious mind.

Those who clearly observe world events will see how the rise and fall of people like Hitler occur. As our subconscious mind gains more power in our life, we go toward destruction. This is true for individuals, nations, and for humanity as a whole.

Imagine how in the name of religion people kill, massacre, and devastate individuals and whole nations. Their religion is great, but their mind is dominated by their subconscious elements so that their religious principles have no power in their life. Their principles are only cosmetic.

People who have fallen under the dominance of their subconscious mind try to use violence against violence, war against war, treason against treason, hatred against hatred. They may win for a short time, but later others take the same actions against them that they took against others in the past. History has many examples for those who know how to read its pages.

It is not easy to realize that you are asleep when you are sleeping. Similarly, it is not easy to see that you are acting under the subconscious mind when you are acting under the subconscious mind. This is the major power of the subconscious mind. But when you begin to awaken, things change.

First, you hate the interference of the subconscious mind. Then you fight against it, trying to be more in control and awake. Third, you overcome it, releasing it in various ways and feeling sick of it. If you awaken one minute a day, five minutes in a month, ten days in a year, you will be a totally transformed person; and before you see the changes in yourself, others will see them first and wonder at how beautiful your life is becoming. If you catch that moment and stretch it, you are on the path of success. This is why observation, self-observation, is such a valuable tool in your hands.

A warning must be given here. **Never expect that your conscious moments will last forever if you do not exercise attention, vigilance, and observation.**

If a person has self-destructive hypnotic suggestions, his behavior shows how he is preparing for self-destruction. For example, take a very happily married couple. One of them has self-destructive suggestions. Whenever the couple reaches a state of success and happiness, the subconscious destructive suggestions of the one partner become active and try to direct him toward circumstances that will lead him into defeat.

Subconscious recordings have such a power that before they get out of hand, they must be detected, controlled, and annihilated.

I knew a girl who, whenever she was happily married, would divorce her husband and go out with a man who fulfilled her subconscious suggestions to live in misery.

One may ask if in the subconscious mind good things also exist. The answer is of course they exist, but they do not last long because the negative ones eat them.

Good things go into the subconscious mind *only when the good and bad are mixed together*. Good things go by themselves into the Chalice. The sewage receives only waste.

There was a girl who came from an alcoholic family. The parents were poor, family relationships were poor, and so on. This girl had a very difficult time with her life and always felt inferior. To protect herself, she used jealousy, gossip, slander, and hatred in her life with others.

One day she bought a new car because she needed one, but still she hated the car. She felt that there was something wrong in having a new car, so she always kept it dirty and full of trash. Once when some friends washed and cleaned the car she felt extremely hurt and angry. She was not comfortable having a new car, nor a successful, decent life. When she began to be successful, the first thing she did was to quit her job. She began to feel more comfortable as her money was spent. Her subconscious mind was telling her that it was wrong to be successful, and she obeyed it.

Once the subconscious mind is controlled, or its behavior clearly observed, a person can find every kind of key to the understanding of human life because the human life is 80%-90% under the power of the subconscious mind.

People inherit their subconscious mind from many, many lives through the recordings of the permanent atoms. People also accumulate certain treasures in their Chalice. The treasure in the Chalice always increases if a person tries to be healthy, happy, prosperous, enlightened, free, and strives toward perfection.

The contents of the subconscious mind suggest just the opposite.

It is interesting that no conflict stands between the Chalice and the subconscious mind until a person is forced to follow spiritual disciplines. At that time a violent reaction starts from the subconscious mind because the person feels very insecure. The subconscious mind realizes that it is totally in danger, so it mobilizes all its power to force itself on the person.

This is observed often in groups and churches when an advancing person suddenly falls into the pit and surrenders himself to the currents of the subconscious mind. During such crises, the only help can come from an experienced Teacher who can explain the situation and prevent the person from sliding back.

This is often impossible when people have the glamor of "freedom of will" and hate to subject themselves to the direction of their Teacher. But if there is trust and love, this can be overcome, and the sanity of the conscious mind can be established.

The period of falling back into the subconscious mind is just like a wheel that is accustomed to turning in the same groove. It will seem pleasurable and natural, and any advice against it will seem to be a violation of "free will."

People think that cycles, new configurations of zodiacal signs and stars bring benevolent changes to humanity. This is a great mistake. No energy from Space can put us into the right direction. On the contrary, it stimulates our beingness at whatever level we may be. And because we are focused mostly in our subconscious mind, we live the same tragic life over and over again as centuries come and go. New cycles, new configurations of stars, new education, and new Teachings can change us only when we respond to them with our conscious mind. Unless we are focused in our conscious mind, we will not benefit from new energies. On the contrary, even with all our sophisticated civilization, we will sink more and more into savagery.[1]

---

1. See also *Cosmic Shocks* and *The Year 2000 & After*.

3 | The Threefold Subconscious

For a long time people have thought that the subconscious mind is related only to the mental body. But the subconscious is not only mental but also emotional and physical. The emotional (or astral) body has its subconscious department into which are accumulated many past recollections and experiences of an emotional nature. The same is true for the physical body, which has its subconscious part.

These subconscious storages emerge in unison when the person is in an advanced stage of development. This is where his problems are. The subconscious elements rush out to the concrete mind from every direction to impose their intentions. When the person begins to advance and he is conscious 25%, only the subconscious part of his physical body surges and controls him. When he advances further, the subconscious parts of the emotional and the physical planes interfere. When he is even more advanced, the physical, emotional, and mental subconsciouses interfere. When he is totally conscious, he is no longer controlled by the subconscious elements since they are all cleaned out. Each of these surge periods is a point of crisis.

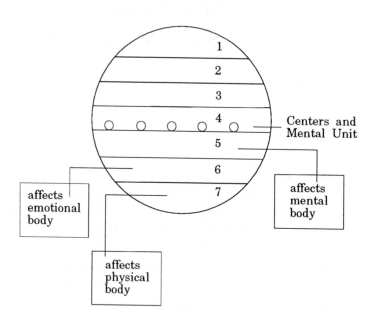

Diagram 3-1 The Threefold Subconscious

Every experience is threefold for the average man. There is the mental element of the experience, there is the emotional element, and there is the physical element. The experience is impressed simultaneously in all three subconsciouses, but they do not interfere with each other if they are not restimulated to the same degree.

For example, the physical subconscious reactivates when it is physically restimulated, the emotional subconscious reactivates when it is emotionally restimulated, and the mental subconscious is reactivated when it is mentally restimulated. When a person is advanced and he is restimulated mentally, the contents of all his emotional and physical subconscious join the "party." This is why as one advances, he has more difficulties to face and he has stronger powers to fight against.

The physical subconscious carries within it all physical experiences. Although the body forgets them or recovers, the impressions are still there. The astral subconscious is mostly full of images of your worship and hate. If fifty years ago you loved a man immensely, his picture is in your astral body. It acts as a presence when it is restimulated. The same is true for someone or something you once hated.

The conscious mind has a very difficult job to clean these "stables." Your astral subconscious is filled especially on occasions of mediumistic activities. Images, entities, and astral corpses not only accumulate there but also slowly devastate your astral body, sucking its energy and paralyzing its activities.

We are told that certain entities from the astral plane are absorbed by our astral body as drops of water are by a sponge. Our movies, television programs, books, and periodicals contribute to our astral subconscious and, when restimulated, they control our life.

This tells us that the human soul has a great task to emancipate himself from this threefold subconscious storage — if he wants to find his true independence.

The mental body has its correspondences in the physical-etheric and astral bodies. Each cell of our physical-etheric body, each atom of our astral body has its own mental plane, of which the seventh, sixth, and fifth subplanes act as its own subconscious mind and resonate with the seventh, sixth, and fifth levels of our mental plane.

It is this mind in the atoms and cells charged by our mental plane, that controls our autonomic nervous system.

The physical subconscious can be controlled by healthy living, good sleep, and deep breathing. The emotional subconscious can be controlled by not exposing yourself to painful, violent movies and programs and by increasing your love and compassion.

The astral subconscious is impressed by what you do to others — but with a twist. For example, if you killed a person, it is recorded in it as if that person were killing you. If you are jealous, it is recorded as if the person you are jealous of were exercising jealousy toward you.

Harmlessness is the key to astral purification. This applies in some degree to the physical subconscious as well.

Regular, rhythmic, and persistent meditation is the highest method to burn out these three subconscious storages.

The astral subconscious can be seen by true clairvoyants. Some people think they see real things, whereas all they see are impressions and illusions. The mental subconscious can be directly visible only to an Arhat, and the physical subconscious can be seen only by a Master. This is very strange, but an intelligent student will find out why.

The mental, astral, and physical subconsciouses are reactivated by similarity of events. They are the part of the memory system of man. A memory can reactivate the elements of these storages.

Someone may ask, "Is it not an advantage to restimulate the subconscious storages so that one sees what is in them?" Of course it is, if you have the power to control bees that are set loose.

Nature is very protective of the human soul. The natural release of such depositories is done very gradually so that the evolving human soul can control them and burn them out. In some sicknesses, all these three storages release elements simultaneously and cause difficulties in the person, leading him almost to insanity.

The mental body, emotional body, and physical body have elementals[1] which have great power over the subconscious elements. In actuality, the elementals hate the subconscious elements because the subconscious elements disturb the neutrality of the elementals. For us, our subconscious elements are images endowed with force. The subconscious elements use the elementals as actors for their drama.

This is the grave danger. If you have an image of a ghost in your subconscious mind, you have a real ghost there because your mental elemental becomes that ghost.

---

1. For further information on elementals, please see *Psyche and Psychism*, Ch. 17, *New Dimensions in Healing*, Ch. 34, and *Other Worlds*, pp. 470-471.

That is why the threefold subconscious nature of man is so powerful. Thus, by polluting your character with violence, hate, anger, jealousy, fear, revenge, and treason, you build ghosts in your subconscious domain and you hinder the development and evolution of your elementals.

Your elementals are your horse, carriage, and reins. Making them useless or nonfunctional prevents you from having the power to use them. But if a person or nation is advanced to a certain degree, the subconscious mind surges out forcefully. This is the reason why humanity is occupied with disease, war, and insanity.

Every harmful action against our elementals makes the elementals react the same way and hurt us.

The subconscious mind itself does not incarnate with the human soul. But, because of the registration in the permanent atoms, the incarnating soul has the weaknesses or tendencies influenced by the recordings corresponding to the subconscious elements.

The subconscious mind begins to form after birth when the recordings in the permanent atoms are heavily restimulated.

This is why every human being has an opportunity not to be limited directly by his past subconscious mind.

It happens also that the elementals incarnate as actors in the drama of our life and become part of it. This is a situation which we witness cyclically upon the earth.

Instead of people incarnating as human souls, their elementals incarnate, representing the human soul. That is how the elementals give back that which the human soul gave to them. This is how karma works.

The Ageless Wisdom teaches that to secure the cooperation of the elementals and help their evolution we must increase our love for all creation. The deeper we love, the more cooperation we find from our threefold elementals. Because they are essentially in tune with Nature, any separative thoughts, feelings, and actions strongly shock them.

4 | The Subconscious and Entities

The subconscious mind has a very close connection with certain entities which are called *elemental spirits* and *elementary spirits*.

The *elemental spirits* are of four kinds. They are evolved from earth, water, air, and fire. They act under the power of the law. People can use them with good or bad motives. This does not matter for them, as they do not have the power to discriminate motives.

These elemental spirits can be drawn to our subconscious dramatizations and ensoul certain parts of the subconscious materials. Then they force the conscious mind to follow blindly what they present.

This happens in a very interesting way. For example, a woman is full of criminal tendencies and scenarios in her subconscious mind. There is a man who hates her. Through the currents of the thoughtforms of hatred, this man unconsciously directs the elementals of air or fire to that woman. Those elementals, driven by the currents of hatred, are attracted to the subconscious thoughtforms of the woman charged with criminal tendencies. The elementals ensoul such subconscious thoughtforms and like to see them dramatized. For example, they flood the consciousness of the woman with destructive imagery and bind her to movements in line with the hatred the man demonstrated toward her.

These elementals cause personal stress and strain. They connect all those people who have common ties with each other and create chaos in their life.

Some elementals love such games because they provide excitement and food.

This was one of the secrets of the advice given by Christ when He said, "*Love your enemies.*" If love is present, elementals do not involve themselves with destructive activities. When we have hatred, malice, and treason, we pull out all the corresponding destructive elements from our subconscious mind and let the elementals ensoul them and play as actors in the dramas of our life.

But the elementals do not do this without taxation. Often they dwell in our lower mental body and create total chaos there, leading us often into criminal actions. They especially love blood, and they do not miss an opportunity, using the hatred of people, to make people shed blood.

Near every drop of human blood, millions of elementals are gathered, and their negative polarity can devastate towns, cities, even continents.

Elementary spirits are astral corpses which are left in the astral plane to decompose. Astral corpses are of two kinds: those which are clean but not evolved enough to burn away immediately when the human soul leaves them and those which are soaked with evil thoughts, emotions, and acts and stay for a long time on the astral plane. These latter become the most dangerous ones when attracted by people who have similar thoughts, emotions, and actions. Sometimes these corpses attach to a person for his entire life, vampirising him, sucking the vitality from his body, emotions, and mind. A time comes when the corpses become the subconscious mind of the person himself and use the contents of the subconscious mind as their nourishment.

A worse thing happens when an earthbound entity, seeing an astral corpse, enters into it and uses it as his emotional body equipped with all the ammunition of destructive thoughts, emotions, and deeds of the astral corpse.

If such an entity possesses a person, that person passes through various stages of consciousness:

1. He yields himself to all destructive tendencies found in his own subconscious mind and in the nature of the astral corpse and its occupant.

Unless he obeys totally the command of the possessor, he will risk his own life because if he opposes for some reason the commands of the possessor, the possessor will destroy the person's mental, emotional, and physical vehicles.

The only way to free oneself from such a possession is to live close to a powerful Teacher who will slowly neutralize the entity and cast it away.

2. The possessed one becomes an instrument through which many such entities are drawn into his environment and are spread to those with whom he is in contact.

Generally, those who live as prostitutes, alcoholics, and drug users, or those who are charged with revenge, hatred, and treason, fall into such a trap. Often these entities follow them life after life, making them miserable during their whole journey.

In order not to attract any such elementals and elementaries, the best attitude to have is to be filled with love, gratitude, forgiveness, and humility. These four virtues attract the benevolent forces of Nature and shield us from any attacks by the unconscious forces of Nature.

Elementals can be controlled and used by powerful Initiates Who have tremendous psychic energy. They use these elementals as electrical currents or forces or energies for constructive purposes.

We are told that some elementals are used by Saints to bring food, to clean rooms, to take messages, and even to discipline some evil people. It is even possible to use them as guards for your windows, gardens, house, or property. They can guard your home better than electrical currents.

Such a power to direct elementals is attained when a person has committed himself to the Common Good of humanity and has gathered enough psychic energy to control or impress them. However, being the neutral agents of Nature, they become destructive if they are used for destructive intentions. No one can escape the damage when he uses them for destructive purposes. In such a case they destroy the agent using them not because of their power of discrimination, which they do not have, but because when they are programmed for destruction, they do their job completely.

It is a pleasure for elemental spirits to play with the contents of the subconscious mind. For us, the contents of the subconscious mind are etheric, emotional, or mental, but for them the contents have an objective existence. They enter into the junkyard of our subconscious mind like children and play with the junk, and if they are directed by us to function in a special way, they do.

Elemental spirits are controlled by many psychics to gather certain secret information that people have. Elemental spirits can read the mind and discover things that were forgotten for decades.

To use the elemental spirits to spy on others and to penetrate into their mental computer turns the elementals against the psychic because the elementals do the same thing to him; they reveal things about him that are secret in his mind.

Arhats or Masters seldom use elemental spirits. They use Their own psychic energy to do things They want to do, but always in harmony with the Supreme Laws of Nature.

5 | Contents of the Subconscious Mind

Most of the contents of the subconscious mind are related to the sixteen elements found in the subconscious mind itself. They are

1. Fear

2. Anger

3. Hatred

4. Jealousy

5. Revenge

6. Slander

7. Malice

8. Treason

9. Vanity

10. Habits

11. Greed

12. Self-interest

13. Superiority

14. Negative imagination

15. Excess sexual urges

16. Subliminal recordings

The subconscious mind begins to record when you are at least 25% unconscious. These sixteen elements, according to their intensity, make you unconscious to a certain degree. All that is associated with these sixteen major elements goes directly into the subconscious mind.

Watch the ocean of events happening around you and in the world, and you will be convinced that the majority of the events are purposeless and anti-survival. These events are eruptions that are rooted in the subconscious mind.

1. Fear is a major element in our subconscious mind. There is fear of death, failure, and defeat; fear of political and economic conditions; fear of sexual violations; fear

collected from our past relationships; fear of insecurity; fear of the unknown, and many other "technicolor" fears.

2. Anger is another element in which we lose all our beauty and equilibrium and try to impose ourselves on others.

3. Hatred is based on racism, on fanaticism, on religious intolerance, on idealism, on jealousy or hurt feelings, on ego, etc.

4. Jealousy is based on an inferiority complex because of the progress of others and the beauty of others, or it may even be the result of being possessed.

5. Revenge is based on past acts of others assumed to be destructive or harmful to us, or it is based on obsession or possession.

6. Slander is based on jealousy, revenge, an inferiority complex, and hatred.

7. Malice is based on our ill thoughts and negative emotions.

8. Treason is mostly based on greed, hatred, and revenge.

9. Vanity is based on ignorance, mental blockages, and an absence of reality in our thoughts.

10. Habits are formed through those circuits in our subconscious mind which force us to repeat certain patterns of behavior.

11. Greed is a sign of not being in contact with the One Self and of being trapped in separatism and fear.

12. Self-interest is the result of evolutionary retardation. Also, it is based on past memories of attacks from various sources.

13. Superiority is a lack of intuitive perception and of being caught in crystallized thoughtforms of ourself.

14. Negative imagination is the result of the release of painful recordings in our subconscious mind. Negative imagination is the use of imagination against Beauty, Goodness, Righteousness, Joy, Freedom, health, and happiness.

15. Excess sexual urges are based on pornographic books or other such publications and movies, being prematurely exposed to sex, or because of ill advice.

16. Subliminal recordings are increasing daily in our subconscious mind. They are mainly coming from some forms of music, advertisements, and political announcements. Subliminal recordings cannot be easily noticed because they go in with the speed of light and sound and immediately begin to germinate in the subconscious mind. We, however, can observe their fruits when they come to the surface.

These sixteen major elements of the subconscious mind, along with hundreds of other related ones, compose what we call the "web of chaos" which is within us. These contents of many colors and intensities force themselves out and periodically surface in our conscious mind with sometimes disastrous consequences.

In the future, great specialists will dare to study this chaos and free humanity from such a nightmare. These specialists will be protected from attacks only because of their pure karma and relatively empty subconscious mind.

We must also remember that these sixteen elements are collected by individuals through their own actions as well as being imposed and forced upon them by others.

These sixteen elements of the subconscious mind are like diskettes which contain all the impressions related to them. At certain times, when more than one element of the subconscious mind is released, they unite together and form a chaotic combination which destroys the sanity, logic, and reasoning of the conscious mind.

Explosions in the subconscious mind can bring either insanity or great release, according to the capacity of the conscious mind to handle them. It is good to remember that the subconscious mind has no permanency.

Often, we try to own a person and make him a slave. But when we fail to do so, we plan how to hurt him. The more we hurt him, the more we fall into fear. The more we are afraid of him, the more we attack him through slander, malice, and treason. Eventually the collected recordings of the subconscious mind start to boil out and lead us into situations in which we realize how far out we went in the ocean of our hatred, jealousy, and treason.

There is a safe distance that we can go and still return to the shore of sanity. But when the distance is too far, it becomes impossible to return. What happens is that either we try to find new shores or we expect the waves of the ocean to destroy us. It is here that the subconscious mind provides all the reasons to go ahead with our desire for self-destruction.

We are advised not to let the winds of our hatred and jealousy push us far into the ocean. Trying to control the life of another person and possess it is the first step taken in the wrong direction. Freedom always ends in joy.

To detach and observe the effects of the subconscious mind is the best method, but one must learn how to observe from various angles and viewpoints.

We can experience that the gradual increase of our viewpoints contributes to our success, happiness, and knowledge. The increase of viewpoints can also lead us into confusion if the process of increasing our viewpoints is not handled wisely.

Here are safeguarding, useful rules:

1. Increase your own viewpoints, and do not borrow the viewpoints of others unless you agree with them.

2. Divide your viewpoints into the following positions:

> personal
>
> family
>
> group
>
> national
>
> global

These are basic viewpoints to keep you in balance.

3. Discriminate between fundamental viewpoints which are physical level viewpoints, emotional level viewpoints, mental level viewpoints, and spiritual level viewpoints.

4. Do not jump from one viewpoint to another until you exhaust the possibilities of at least two of your viewpoints.

5. Notice that some viewpoints are opposites, contradictory, or alternative, depending on your basic or fundamental viewpoints.

6. Observe that essential viewpoints are past, present, and future.

7. Try to create a viewpoint that can be named the viewpoint of the future.

These are only suggestions. You can find other viewpoints that will ease the work of detaching yourself from the function of your subconscious mind in your daily activities.

6 | The Subconscious and Hypnotic States

We are in a hypnotic state every time our consciousness is dimmed to a certain degree. The diminution of consciousness takes place when

1. We are defeated in some way

2. We feel that we have failed

3. We are depressed

4. We are sick or in fever

5. We are in pain or wounded

6. We watch violence and identify with it

7. We witness murder

8. Our mind is in suspension

9. We are extremely happy

10. We are irritated or caught in intense hatred, fear, jealousy, malice

11. We act against our conscience

12. We harm people

13. We have just awakened

14. We have just fallen asleep

15. We act as a hypocrite

16. We are attacked by someone's anger

These are the main moments that create a hypnotic state in our consciousness, so it is very important that shocks are not given to us in the form of bad news or upsetting statements. During these times the consciousness dims to a considerable degree. The mental unit, which is a very sensitive mechanism, shuts itself and leaves the door open to the subconscious mind.

The mental unit acts as the watch between the conscious and the subconscious mind. When the consciousness diminishes, it immediately affects the mental unit. But if the mental unit is connected to the mental permanent atom, hypnotism becomes an impossibility.

Besides the danger of hypnotism, there is the danger of shocks. If a highly evolved person is in trance, sudden noise or low level vibration emanating from people creates disturbances and even shocks in his subtle bodies.

My Teacher used to go and meditate in a special cave which was prepared for him. No one was allowed to go there when he was in meditation.

Once I asked why such a caution. I was told, "During meditation he is abstracted, and any noise or visit by people may give a shock to his nervous system or to his subtle bodies."

For a long time students should avoid all possibilities of shocks during their meditation such as telephone calls, various noises, interference from people, and so on.

There are moments in our meditation or contemplation when suspension occurs in our consciousness in which we have no control over our mental mechanism. Suspension is the sleep of consciousness. This happens when the accumulated elements in the subconscious try to interfere and control our present life and also affect our future.[1]

The contents of the subconscious mind interfere with our plans as often as our karma does with our life.

For example, if in a past life you made money by illegal means and you had a terrible time with the law or with your conscience, your subconscious mind may lead you into a condition in this life in which you hate money, or you hate making money, and choose to live a life of poverty though unconscious about the causes of it.

---

1. For more information on meditation, see *The Science of Meditation, The Psyche and Psychism,* and *The Ageless Wisdom.*

Similar things happen if one misuses his sex energy, involving himself (or herself) with many problems. Those who hate sex and are by nature frigid are those who in the past were loaded with fear and resentment. It is possible to help such people through certain psychological exercises not known to present day psychologists.

Most of the negative situations we are in are an indication that either we violated the law, or we misused the gifts of life in many ways.

Once I asked a beggar who was extremely intelligent, "With such an intelligence to create a good life for yourself, for others, why with ragged clothes do you beg in the street?"

"Dear One," he said, "you cannot understand. I hate to have more than I need, and I hate to work for money. It gives me extreme pain."

All such cases can be cured if the causes are understood.

Every time we violate the law and create fear in us or hurt our conscience, the hypnotic suggestion penetrates into our subconscious mind, providing a record for karma to act through.

7 | The Subconscious Mind and Good Things

The subconscious mind also contains good things when the good is related to pain, suffering, worry, anxiety, and grief. When you recall the good memories, instead of joy or success, you feel pain and are led to failure. How does this happen? Suppose your father gave you a football, and your brother beat you and took the football away from you. From that moment on, whenever you wish to have a football, you will be reminded of the pain.

A young man married a beautiful girl. One day, when they were very happy, four people came and killed the girl. From that moment on, a beautiful girl meant death to that man.

Or, when listening to great music in a theater, an earthquake strikes and kills five hundred people in the audience. You then hate to go to theaters or even listen to great music anymore because that subconscious memory is restimulated.

Any good memories associated with pain and suffering cause trouble in your life.

A gentleman once told me that the worst thing that could happen to him was success because every time he became successful, jealous and revengeful people in his family destroyed his job. Now he is afraid of success and tries to live a poor man's life to avoid trouble.

There are events recorded in your subconscious mind that force you to involve yourself in situations that give you both joy and suffering. For example, an artist came to my office and complained that her husband was beating her and she was beating him. Then they would make love because both were very anxious to make love. The husband died one day, and the artist began to date many men.

Once I asked her, "When are you going to marry?" She answered, "I cannot marry these smart, polite gentlemen. I can't enjoy them. There is something wrong in the way they relate to me."

Eventually, she found a man just like her previous husband. He began to beat her. They lived together for seven years, fighting and making love everyday. One day I read in the newspaper that the husband had killed her.

The subconscious mind controls your life, and it becomes highly dangerous for you if there are recordings in it that are joyful and painful at the same time because you live in permanent confusion and indecisiveness.

8 | The Subconscious Mind and Dreams

Our subconscious mind manifests itself also through dreams. Most of our dreams dramatize the elements we have in our subconscious mind. Studying and analyzing such dreams help us partially to know the contents of our subconscious mind.

In the subconscious mind, we also have certain elements that are not the recordings of past events but are our desires, daydreams, and wishes dramatized by our imagination while we were not 100% awake. Our consciousness can suppress for a while our wild desires, daydreams, and wishes, but a day comes when the subconscious mind can no longer be imprisoned. Our desires, daydreams, and wishes come to the surface, either through dreams or through strong blind urges and drives.

This is Nature's way of reducing pressure that is building in the subconscious mind.

Sometimes dreams save us from being victims of our wild desires and wishes. If the subconscious pressures do not express themselves through dreams, we often become the victims of the surging currents of our subconscious elements.

It is very interesting to note that all our daydreams, wishes, and desires accumulate in our subconscious mind, which in turn helps us actualize them. But such an actualization carries certain dangers with it, due to various associations with unpleasant subconscious elements which act without consideration for the state in which the person lives.

For example, suppose you desire another woman while you are married. This desire goes into your subconscious mind and slowly increases in strength and makes you find the ways and means to fulfill your desire. You fulfill your desire, but you see that certain complications emerge in your consciousness and conscience. The subconscious mind releases elements that make your romance powerful. At the same time it reminds you of past associations and their results. And if you continue your romance, you complicate your situation even more.

Some people decide to stop before it is too late, but the process of separation creates abundant subconscious elements which sink, recycle, and come back to the surface of their mind any time they think about the woman. This is why the Sages advise us not to put ourselves in situations which, because of negative emotions, anger, and fear, increase the contents of our subconscious mind. They suggest that we live an innocent and conscious life.

The contents of the subconscious mind are different from the thoughtforms of our aspirations and good wishes in that the latter are of a higher caliber. The difference is that such thoughtforms are pure and progressive, whereas the recordings in the subconscious mind are mixed with many kinds of contradictory materials.

The conflict between these two factors sometimes is very painful because, when the thoughtforms try to actualize themselves, the subconscious recordings interfere and "whisper" to the conscious mind that "the actualization of these thoughtforms may bring pain and suffering with them," and the conclusion is that "you must be very careful." Hesitation and confusion are fruits of such situations.

The interesting point is that nothing stays separate in the subconscious mind. Anything recorded in it is immediately related to something else that has a certain relationship with it. For example, if an event is very joyful and that event was celebrated with candles, the subconscious computer searches and finds an event that has no relation with that event at all, except that a candle was involved. With the link of the candle, these two chains are joined together and they manifest as one event.

Some intelligent people, endowed with analytic power, are able to analyze these two events to discover the link existing between them.

Some of the movies and programs that children are watching on television are fabrications of people who are under the influence of their subconscious mind. Ugliness, violence, murder, and horror are mixed with happy moments and wise words and are put in almost all our movies. People enjoy this subconscious trash and support the people who make such films so that the dumping of this subconscious trash into our lives is continued.

9 | Habits and the Subconscious Mind

Habits are subconscious circuits that affect your etheric body and control your life until one day someone or some event awakens you and you break your habit. There are so many habits — eating habits, sex habits, Friday night habits, drinking habits, doping habits, sleeping habits — and many more. For example, if you do not go out to dinner on Friday night with your boyfriend or girlfriend, it is the end of the world for you. Unless you control and then master your habits, you cannot become a self-actualized, self-determined human being. The whole intention of the subconscious mind is to rule your life.

Progress is made when habits are decreased. That is why we are told that whenever we are building a habit, we must stop and put an end to it. Even some good things that we do by habit do not build our spirituality nor help us advance.

You feel nervous and irritated because on your birthday you expected flowers, but they did not come. Your subconscious mind makes you feel uneasy, "arguing" with you and urging you to have the flowers, the card, the gift. If they do not come, you lose your equilibrium.

The best way to conquer such situations is to observe yourself as if you were someone else observing this person who is full of expectation and irritation. If you cannot see your habits or stop them, it means you are the slave of your subconscious mind. There are physical habits, emotional habits, and mental habits.

When you develop the power of observation, you will see that on certain occasions you are reacting in the same way as in the past; you are thinking in the same way and talking in the same way. When you notice this, you will have great success in your spiritual life.

Suppose your mother came and pulled your ear and said, "You are stupid! I told you a hundred times you are not going to be a human being. Do you understand?" This is a very complicated suggestion which sinks into the subconscious mind because of its painful quality.

Later in life, when this event is restimulated, you program your life in a way that you act stupidly, and you do all that is possible not to act like a human being. You will destroy your life if you do not get rid of such dangerous suggestions.

The push-buttons of such an event are

— ears

— fingers

— mother's voice

— mother

— hundred times

— not a human being

— Do you understand?

— I told you

— the air

— the smell

— the environment

Subconscious events have hundreds of tails by which they can be brought into action. People whose subconscious mind has been restimulated are called prisoners. There are millions of people who are endowed with many talents, but their talents and beauty are locked inside subconscious caves.

One of the great services of disciples is to free such people and let humanity benefit from their talents.

Some people wonder why we have both the Chalice and the subconscious mind. What are they? How can we use them?

The Chalice is the treasury, the storage of things you do not need immediately in your life. It is not easy to approach the Chalice, but it is very easy to contact or cause a release from the subconscious mind since the subconscious mind functions through associations.

The Chalice is in the higher mind, and, in general, there is no bridge to reach it. First, you must build a bridge between the mental unit and the Mental Permanent Atom via the center of the Chalice. This means you must be a somewhat evolved human being to reach the treasury. Before you are ready, the treasures in the Chalice will be very dangerous for you to have under your possession.

The relation between the Chalice and the subconscious mind is that eventually the Chalice uses all the elements in the subconscious mind as partial food for its growth.

As the Chalice or the Lotus unfolds, it draws the contents of the subconscious mind, piece by piece, and transforms them into knowledge and experience. In transforming the contents into knowledge and experience, these contents of the subconscious mind decrease and eventually vanish. After each accumulation of the subconscious mind changes into knowledge and experience, it adds to the treasury of the Chalice and contributes to the growth of the petals of the Chalice. Thus, nothing is wasted in the Universe.

Through meditation, the mechanism of the Chalice pulls out the threads of many accumulations, exposes them as they are, reveals their causes and the process of how and why they came into being, under what laws they were accumulated, and under what laws they can be recycled and used as sources of knowledge, experience, and wisdom.

As the petals of the Chalice open and expand, the subconscious mind slowly fades. The conscious mind, or the Light of Consciousness, penetrates not only the fifth, sixth, and seventh levels of the mind, but it also begins to penetrate into the higher mind, which includes the third, second, and first levels. When the subconscious mind fades, the physical and astral bodies begin to function completely according to the plan of the first and second levels of the higher mind.

Thus, when the nine petals of the Chalice are finally open and the innermost petals begin to unfold, the consciousness uses the entire seven levels of the mind as a unified field of light and achieves mental, emotional, and etheric synthesis. The three permanent atoms at the base of the Lotus begin to radiate like diamonds, and the network of communications within the three bodies reaches perfection.[1]

Illumination is the period in which the petals of the Chalice, flooded with the fire of the Central Core, release the light of each atom of the three lower bodies, and the threefold man shines like a diamond.

Each petal of the Chalice has its specialized labor in relation to the subconscious mind. The contents of the subconscious mind related to knowledge, love, and sacrifice exist in a reversed, contaminated, and twisted manner. There is "gold" in all of them but wrapped in pain, suffering, hate, anger, vanity, ego, exploitation, manipulation, greed, revenge, jealousy, and selfishness. But the refinery of the Chalice knows how to change alchemically these elements into the gold of wisdom.

We increase the contents of the subconscious mind not only during our unconscious moments but also when

---

1. For a fuller description of the constitution of man, please refer to *New Dimensions in Healing* and *The Science of Becoming Oneself.*

we lie and fabricate things to others and especially to ourselves. When we lie to others, the lie penetrates into our subconscious mind, but the truth around the lie goes to the Chalice. Then a contradictory situation is created between these two containers, while in the meantime a subjective link is created between them. This is what self-deception is.

Self-deception forms a cloud which floats in the conscious mind, hindering its proper functions. As it increases in size and permanency, it lasts a long time, and it sinks into the subconscious mind. At proper occasions the subconscious mind uses these self-deceptions to control the life of the person. Thus, those who have fallen into self-deception do not realize that in the future their life will be controlled not by reality but by the falsehood that they had previously created.

10 | Blackouts

Another very mysterious element in the subconscious mind is called a "blackout." This is a moment in which you freeze or black out when you see certain colors, hear certain words, etc. When, for example, you hear a word that really frightened you, in that moment you experience a gap in consciousness, a momentary blackout. You feel mentally paralyzed.

These words and other signals are related to natural catastrophes, murders, or various horrors. They create very dangerous moments which, when activated, make your consciousness blank. Many car accidents and many accidents at work are caused by such blank moments.

The moments of blacking out are different in nature. For example, while listening to someone, a moment comes when you hear nothing and you miss some valuable information or an order that was given. Another moment of blacking out is experienced when you totally forget something, for instance, a word you intended to say. Blackouts become more dangerous when you are driving on the freeway or when you are operating dangerous machinery.

Such moments are not easy to observe. But if you practice observation and question yourself after the moment of blacking out, in a few years you will begin to make a breakthrough.

I had a friend who was waiting for a medical report. The doctor came and told him that the tests were positive and that he had malignant cancer. We found out later that it was a mistaken report, but after that incident this man blacked out every time the words "positive," "doctors," "hospital," or "cancer" were used.

Accumulations of such moments can have drastic results. Blackouts can damage the brain and cause great harm to the person and his future. Self-analysis or psychoanalysis cannot dissolve such moments. It is only through meditation that this problem can be solved.[1]

Meditation is an organizing factor. It organizes the body, the emotions, and the mind and eventually builds the network of the Antahkarana in all the personality vehicles. Wherever there is continuity, gaps disappear.

---

1. Please refer to *The Science of Meditation, The Psyche and Psychism*, and *The Ageless Wisdom* for information on proper meditation.

11 | The Subconscious and Impressions

It must be clear in our mind that the subconscious mind registers impressions only if in some way the conscious mind falls into sleep or is absent.

The conscious mind can be absent when in certain conditions the human soul is pushed away from the mental body or when the mental body is occupied by an obsessor. If the obsessor is an entity, we call it possession. If the obsessor is a thoughtform, we call it obsession. In both cases we notice a short or long period in which the consciousness is absent.

Obsession occurs also in certain accidents during which the soul withdraws from the physical body. For instance, it may occur when a man is knocked out from a blow on his head or spine.

It is in these absent moments that most of the impressions enter into the subconscious and change into posthypnotic suggestions or blind urges and drives.

The conscious mind sleeps or becomes absent also when the person loses himself in certain moments of extreme happiness or in moments when his mind is totally abstracted in another direction.

Many painful conditions and extreme suffering and pain considerably diminish the light of consciousness and make man prey to posthypnotic suggestions.

The restimulation of the subconscious mind also needs certain conditions in which the conscious mind is in some degree abstracted.

It is possible also that certain impressions reach the subconscious mind in the form of subliminal suggestions when the person is not 100% awake. Worries, anxieties, irritation, hatred, anger, jealousy, greed, and fear are open doors for subliminal suggestions.

Any element that enters the subconscious mind makes the subconscious computer work and makes the element fit into the chains of existing recordings.

Every time the subconscious mind is restimulated, some elements in it are violently stimulated and others are pacified. Those impressions that are related to emotional disturbances due to sickness, death, divorce, and so on, create agitations. Those which are related to fear create a cooling or freezing effect.

Restimulated elements in the subconscious mind accumulate energy and try to express themselves in various ways.

This is now becoming a mass-control system which, if not stopped, will be used to manipulate the world for certain private and sectarian interests.

Subliminal suggestions will create a world in which people will not only fight within themselves but also fight with each other, creating world chaos.

The solution is to raise your consciousness, to expand it to such a degree that you are always conscious. You must try to keep your balance and have divine indifference so as not to be angry, not to hate, not to criticize, not to be afraid, not to be excited overwhelmingly, not to be suspended, but to be conscious and in contact with reality.

It is also evident that drug users, alcohol users, even tobacco and black tea and coffee users lose their consciousness to a certain degree and accept very destructive suggestions into their subconscious mind.

Marijuana fails the consciousness to a great degree, and the person becomes sensitive not only to subliminal suggestions but also to any outer suggestions which turn within him into posthypnotic suggestions.

Drug users especially are bombarded with negative subliminal suggestions. That is why they commit so many crimes.

People speak about prejudices or about superstitions. Most of such formations are built in our subconscious throughout the years around a posthypnotic nucleus in our subconscious mind.

Superstitions and prejudices are mighty thoughtforms floating in the pool of our subconscious mind and controlling our thinking, decisions, directions, and relationships.

They have a mighty power once they are in operation. Once they are recognized for exactly what they are, they lose all their power. Such recognition comes through a moment of enlightenment, when a beam of intuitional light hits the thoughtform.

Most prejudices and superstitions are built around the nucleus of a lie which has the elements of emotion and logic.

Prejudices and superstitions block the path of progress of people. These grow in religious, educational, and social fields and exercise a great power to restrict the expansion of consciousness and right human relations.

What we call fanaticism is a thoughtform built upon a solid nucleus, but grown by wrong, selfish intentions and motives.

Any solid nucleus, when used by wrong, selfish intentions to exploit others, to impose their will or ideas on others, and to manipulate them, builds a blind thoughtform of fanaticism which not only destroys others but also the owner himself — whether individual, group, or nation.

Consciousness, when in a state of expansion, penetrates not only into higher planes but also into the lower planes of the mind. The expansion of consciousness produces the unity of all the levels of the mental plane.

In this process of expansion, from the center of the conscious mind the light of consciousness penetrates into the higher and lower minds. This light sheds its radiation into the fifth level and the third level and goes further and further in an ever inclusive circle on the mental plane.

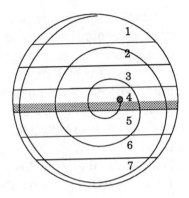

Diagram 11-1 Expansion of Consciousness

When the light of consciousness penetrates into the fifth level of the mental plane, it slowly releases the locked subconscious impressions that are also the contents of the fifth plane. These impressions become for the person a storehouse of significant memories collected during the "absence" of consciousness.

The fifth level of mind is used as a mine by geniuses in their creative work. But remember that as the consciousness expands into the fifth level, it is also expanding into the third level, into the abstract mind, which is the most creative level of the mind, used to build artistic palaces out of the ink mine of the fifth level subconscious mind.

The fifth level of the mind contains experiences and rare recordings that had bypassed our conscious mind. The person, as he discovers these treasures and sorts the rubbish from the gold, finds the best experiences with which to build castles or to discover the reasons, laws, and causes of much of his behavior unknown to him before.

These subconscious elements are used by artists and scientists to create far reaching literature and discoveries.

Many great artists use the elements of the fifth level of mind to create magnificent literature, as did Dostoyevsky, Goethe, Milton, Chekhov, Rabindranath Tagore, and others. They would consciously enter into their own subconscious mind and select those experiences that fit their artistic labor.

As one advances on the Path, his consciousness expands into the second and first levels of the mind and into the sixth and seventh levels of the mind, and eventually the mental plane turns into a unified field of light. This is what we call the state of real Illumination. The fire of the Chalice increases and causes transmutation in all subconscious material.

As the unification and fusion of the mental plane goes on, the incarnations of the soul improve and he takes birth in those locations where he can radiate his light and become an instrument of great service, love, power, and freedom. Then, through the illumination of the subconscious mind, man discovers his path toward greater freedom of health, happiness, prosperity, and service.

Such a transmutation process strongly affects the health of the person. Most of the tensions existing in the mental body become lighter. The pressure exercised by the contents of the subconscious mind over the body organs and over etheric and astral chakras becomes less and less, and the person experiences a tremendous release.

Of course, those who have fewer subconscious elements will be born with better bodies because their lower permanent atoms will have fewer seeds of distortion for future bodies.

It is known that if a person is loaded with subconscious elements he is not considered a good candidate for advanced spiritual work or for high level public work.

Advanced spiritual work demands that one come in contact with higher centers of force and with fiery energies. As these fires and energies flow into his mental field, they may cause what is called esoterically "destruction of the subconscious dam." The strong and suppressed urges and drives find opportunity to be released, and they flood the life of the person and make him do things he never imagined doing.

For example, if the flood is related to sex elements, the person finds himself doing things that totally violate the law, his conscience, and rules of society, and he merges into a sexual life that destroys his credibility, his relationships, and his future.

If the flood is related to greed, then he cheats, deceives, manipulates, and destroys his future after trying to build it.

This appears in all fields of human endeavor when suddenly an honest person does the most obnoxious things, creating massive confusion.

We are told that we have seven major dams in our subconscious system, each related to one of seven major complexes: sex, food, money, revenge, love of possessions, manipulation, exploitation. If these areas in the subconscious mind are restimulated, the dams will break and the person will find himself in a very humiliating situation unless an advanced Teacher offers his help.

Invoking higher energies and forces, or being close to those people who are charged with a great amount of fiery energies, even visiting places which are reservoirs of energies can cause cracks in the "dams," eventually destroying them totally and letting the flood destroy all that the person built.

Sages very intelligently discriminate the condition of their disciples before they kindle their energy centers and impart the fiery Teaching so as not to cause flooding or an explosion within their subconscious storages.

People do not realize what a tragic effect destructive news has on their consciousness. We are constantly bombarded by news of crime, violence, and accidents, which is filling our subconscious day and night and conditioning our thinking, feeling, and actions to a considerable degree.

Why must everyone know with detailed description about the criminal who annihilated ten people?

Why must everyone see pictures of ragged bodies from an explosion that killed two hundred people?

A child who listens to all this news will be a failure in society.

Most of us are falling victim to the violence and crime especially going on in government circles.

Of course crimes, accidents, and violence must be recorded, and people who want to know for specific purposes and service can know, but why force every ugly and dirty and bloody event into the throats of people, and for what reason except to create total chaos in the minds of average people?

How many tons of trash are dumped into the subconscious of our youth?

One teenager while I was talking with her said, "What is the use of education and morality? Everybody is a crook from the highest to the lowest level. Crime is everywhere. Violence and butchering are legal jobs. I don't even want to live in such a society."

We and our children are fed-up with crime and ugliness from the top level to the bottom. What vision is our media giving to people in America and to the world?

All the subconscious trash accumulated in our mind is gradually surfacing. The proof is the increasing crimes and failures of the youth.

The flood of subconscious elements attack those areas in the human consciousness which resist the flood or try to hinder its course. If the hindrances are found in his value system, they destroy it. If the hindrance is found in the glandular or nervous system, the flood wipes it away causing widespread effects.

If the hindrances are found in the field of feelings and emotions, the flood may possibly hit the heart and blood stream, and if the hindrances are in the field of desires, the flood hits the digestive system or the sexual organs.

If the hindrances are on the emotional plane, the flood hits the lungs. Thus those who are involved with higher energies without due preparation suffer in various ways until they clean the hindrances.

The lives of many important people can stand as witness for all the above information.

The contents of the subconscious mind are charged with etheric, astral, and mental forces. Sometimes the elements are only mental or astral or etheric. Sometimes they are combinations. When this is the case, any cleaning process meets many difficulties.

A newborn baby inherits all the shocks that a mother receives from physical, emotional, and mental realms. The baby receives all the effects of the subconscious eruptions of the mother. People in the past thought that we could use our subconscious mind to influence our body. The fact is that we can directly influence our body through our conscious mind, through creative imagination and visualization, and through charging it with higher energies.

Our etheric body, which is the energy field of our physical body, is sensitive to all our thoughts, emotions, and actions, and all these are conditioning factors of our physical body. Some people have developed a tremendous control over their physical body through their etheric body. They can even slow and change the palpitation of their heart, or stop blood flowing from a wound. Such powers can be developed if the subconscious mind is mostly wiped out.

12 | How the Subconscious Elements Surface

The subconscious elements come to the surface

1. When they are associated with stimulation coming from the outer world such as television programs, reading, advertisements, and commercials

2. Through imagination

3. When the influence of dark forces exercises pressure

4. During dreams

5. During times of crises

6. During fever or sickness

7. Through the art of obsession

8. During the cleansing process by the Chalice

9. During sudden explosions

10. During periods of certain full moons

11. When meeting or being with someone whose subconscious mind resonates with the contents of yours

12. When imbalance in the chemical substances in the brain causes elements from the subconscious to escape into the conscious mind

To be free from stimulation and to act consciously in our life means to be less limited by our subconscious mind and to be awake.

Nature often offers us a few seconds to see the abyss of our subconscious mind, and we must be cautious not to fall into the abyss. The elements of the subconscious mind cannot stay very long under the pressure of the logical mind, under rules, orders, and regulations. They will often erupt like a volcano, destroying all the protective walls of the logical mind and customary and traditional behavior.

The reason for this is that thoughtforms in our subconscious mind are built of fiery elements that operate under the law of expansion. The atoms of these elements are in constant motion and radioactivity. They exert tremendous pressure upon the logical mind and force their way out, sometimes through bribing the logical mind,

13 | Emotions and the Subconscious Mind

The subconsciousness has a very close relation with our astral body. The etheric body is controlled by our *lower mental plane*, namely by the seventh, sixth, fifth, and fourth levels of the mind, but our etheric body also has a close relation with the astral body through the seven centers in the astral body.

The subconscious elements in our lower mental body affect our astral body as a whole through the etheric body. This is why most of the subconscious elements first appear in our emotional moods or emotional states before they are formulated into thought.

If we closely follow the changes, fluctuations, stimulation, and excitement of our emotional body, we can have a fair idea about the contents of our subconscious mind.

Our emotions reveal the secret of our subconscious mind, but we do not pay attention to them. The emotional body often acts as a safety valve to relax the pressure accumulating in the subconscious mind.

It is also true that by exercising mastery over our emotions we consciously affect our subconscious mind and body. Consciously changing our emotional states changes or annihilates many subconscious elements in our nature, which in turn introduce changes in our physical body as well.

At the beginning of human evolution, we had only the seventh level of the mental body active. Our subconscious mind and conscious mind were one. We were mostly mechanically controlled. The impressions collected in the seventh layer were factors to put us in motion.

As we advanced, the sixth level of the mental body began to be active, and twenty-five percent of our active mind detached itself from the seventh layer of the mind. As we advanced more, the whole seventh layer and one fourth of the sixth layer began to act as the subconscious mind, and the fifth layer of the mind began to be our conscious mind.

In the Fourth Root Race, the sixth and seventh layers of the mind became our subconscious mind, and we penetrated into the first level of the mind.

In the Fifth Race, the Aryan Race, our consciousness is focused now in the fourth level of the mind, and the fifth, sixth, and seventh levels act as subconscious mind.

As disciples and initiates advance, they enter into the third level or the abstract level of the mind, and, in the meantime, clean the fifth level of the mind and make it part of the fourth level of the mind, the conscious mind.

As they advance into the second level and the first level of the abstract mind, they purify the sixth level and the seventh level of the mind from all their subconscious accumulations and make them part of the conscious mind. This is called the state of *awakeness*.

When an Initiate focuses his consciousness on the Intuitional Plane, all mental levels turn into an organized field of the conscious mind. The man is then totally awake, liberated, and free.

Thus, the mental body becomes clean and reflects the Higher Worlds.

14 | Releases of the Subconscious Mind

There are times in your life when your subconscious mind releases itself in some degree, for example between the ages of

14 - 18

27 - 35

42 - 49

53 - 62

65 - 70

72 - 80

During these years you feel a subconscious surge and are challenged to take action in order to control it. If you do not control it by age 49, as you get older, especially after age 62, your subconscious mind may release itself in your dreams, awaken you at 2:00 or 3:00 a.m., and release so much fear and ugliness from your past life that you are bathed in sweat.

Before you pass away, you must gain a great deal of control over the subconscious mind. The subconscious mind can travel with you in the Subtle Worlds and create many difficulties on your journey. However, it does not return with you in a new incarnation because it burns away in the Fiery World. But, because of the existence of recordings in the three permanent atoms, the subconscious mind quickly builds its separate domain once again. The building generally starts after age seven.

The Chalice always stays with us. If it is unfolded and radiant, we enjoy the Subtle World a great deal.

Some people are presently using visualization techniques to overcome subconscious drives. One of my friends wrote me a letter and asked, "There is a young man who is going berserk when I ask him to visualize a lily. What do you think is causing it?" Before I answered her letter, I spoke to the young man who was visiting me at the time. I said, "Did you lose any of your family members?"

"Yes."

"Who was it?"

"My mother."

"Were there many kinds of flowers at the funeral?"

"There were many flowers," and he became red in the face, "but they were all white lilies."

"What kind of car do you have?"

"A Volvo."

"Do you like it?"

"Yes."

Then I told him how many Volvos I had bought, repaired, and sold — just to drive his mind away from the white lilies. Later I wrote to my friend, "Before you give any form of visualization, try to find out if it is related to painful memories. If yes, never present it until you learn how to handle adverse situations." Immediately when the subject was to visualize a lily, the boy's consciousness faded and he fell into the subconsciousness where the event was registered with all its physical pain, emotional suffering, and mental anxiety.

To help clean the subconscious mind through visualization is a dangerous art. You cannot use wholesale practices that you borrow from irresponsible people.

The difficulty of knowing when you are acting under the subconscious mind is magnified when you are identified with your subconscious mind in a large percentage. That is where its strength lies. Once you are identified, you think that whatever you are thinking, saying, or doing is done by you. Sometimes you are lucky. You hesitate to do what you want to do, or after you do it you hate yourself. If such hesitation and self-criticism go on for a few minutes without rationalizing them away, we say that there is hope for you since you may realize that it is not you but your subconscious mind directing your actions. But if you cannot make a breakthrough, you fall under the dominance of the subconscious mind even more than you did before. Realization makes you have power over it, and with the help of the Teacher you can conquer it.

There is a layer in the subconscious mind that collects many kinds of philosophies, religions, and traditions that were given to the person when he was not ready to understand them, or when he was in some degree unconscious or sick or desperate. This is the origin of what are called glamor and illusion.

For example, when you were sick your mother read some religious stories, some philosophy, and occasionally said to you that "in the future you will teach all this to people." All such moments go to a layer of the subconscious mind, and in the future when they are restimulated, you build a glamor for yourself and think that you are a great teacher. You try to "prove" this by imitating whatever is found in your subconscious mind.

Many, many lives are ruined by planting in them such glamors. This is why in some esoteric schools you can attend a class only if you are really awake so that the Teaching does not become part of your subconscious mind.

First, things that are in the subconscious mind are not part of your beingness, and when you are under its influence, you are imitating and pretending and being a hypocrite.

Second, if you are not ready for the role you are going to play, you put yourself under severe stress. Your glamors use and direct your energies without any good results. Most of the degeneration of the Teaching begins and ends in such a manner. You act like a soldier, a teacher, or a president. You are cosmetically built; you are artificial. And once you fall into that role, it is very difficult to get out of it.

Third, glamors, because they are associated with the subconscious mind, eventually wear down and degenerate. A glamor is a form which sometimes decays and pollutes all your approaches to life. Most of the degeneration of the Teaching is due to this. Glamors act both in the astral and mental levels. A glamor can be mentalized and become a mental glamor. Illusions come into being when a fact is mixed up with glamors.

For example, a girl was always told that she was a holy angel. At age seventeen, she had her first sexual experience. Then she joined a club where sexual freedom was a common practice. Eventually she became a prostitute. But, because she was "a holy angel," she continuously slandered good girls in her neighborhood and called them many bad names. No matter what she did, she felt she was "a holy angel."

Such people are great problems and their salvation depends on those who sincerely, frankly, openly, and tactfully tell them what they really are and how they became that way.

Everything that you have, if it is not the fruit of your labor, is a hindrance in your life and a potential danger. Only the things that you accumulate in the Chalice with your striving, labor, sweat, and sincerity belong to you. The rest is like ornamentation on an ugly body. But people like to ornament themselves with the feathers of peacocks rather than work hard to be beautiful.

It is very difficult to break a glamor, which is built during your unconscious moments by your wishes and desires. Greed is a terrible glamor. Love of possessions of every kind is almost an evil urge.

Because of greed, people remain deaf to the whispers of their Inner Guide and cheat people and deceive them to accumulate money or possessions.

Every penny taken from people through deceiving, manipulating, and frightening them will turn into a debt in the Subtle World and in the next life will have terrible consequences. Christ said, "Give therefore to Caesar what is Caesar's, and to God what is God's,"[1] which means do not take things that do not belong to you.

But of course the subconscious mind has thousands of cards to play with and win. We call them rationalizations, justifications, and legalities. Once your subconscious mind makes your stupidity legal, there will be no hope for you.

The more you unfold your Chalice, the less subconsciousness you have, and eventually you become 50% conscious and 50% subconscious. Now which one is going to grow and win? That decision will come from your karma. If in the past you sowed seeds of service and sacrifice, your karma will lead you to the right books and right teachers so that your consciousness grows and expands.

When Christ said, "But I say to you who hear, Love your enemies and do good to those who hate you,"[2] He meant do not act under the subconsciousness. "Whoever asks from you, give to him; and whoever wishes to borrow from you, do not refuse him."[3] The subconscious mind says, do not give anything except if they give you something. Such an attitude has been built within us.

"Love your enemies, bless anyone who curses you, do good to anyone who hates you, and pray for those who carry you away by force and persecute you."[4] The sub-

---

1. Matt. 22:21
2. Luke 6:27
3. Matt. 5:42
4. Matt. 5:44

conscious mind will immediately interfere and say, "They persecuted you; you must persecute them."

Acting under the subconscious mind perpetuates your karma and results in a vicious circle. Someone must stop it and act under the conscious mind to break this vicious circle.

For Christ, it was better to be in the conscious mind than to be identified with the subconscious mind which believes in "an eye for an eye."

It is understanding and love that help us make a breakthrough and help us choose to stay in the conscious mind. The conscious mind arranges things by favoring all those who are not contaminated by the subconscious mind.

15 | Self-Punishment

The subconscious mind provides all the materials and urges to make a man punish himself.

Occasionally, through the law of association, painful recordings come up to the conscious mind and make people re-experience past traumas.

Many nightmares are the result of such restimulations. This is a self-punishment technique in which echoes of past deeds come again and again to hit you. Such recordings do not stay in their original size but grow enormously by attracting piles of recordings that have some affinity with them.

In this state of mind, you may tune to the subconscious minds of other people and draw to your subconscious mind their own problems.

The subconscious mind plays a big role in your mental condition. If it is not handled correctly, it may lead you to mental and physical diseases or even to suicide. The ancients had a very good method to fight against such conditions: fasting and continuous praying.

If right psychological conditions are created by fasting and praying, it may be possible that your subconscious mind will receive a beam of light which in turn will destroy the accumulated recordings and annihilate them.

Confession is another method to clean your subconscious mind. Also, if you have a loving person around you, his or her psychic energy can eliminate many recordings.

It is also possible to help yourself through your creative imagination, imagining exactly the opposite of your recordings. For example, if your subconscious mind is suggesting that you are going to fail, be defeated, lose your wife or husband, or commit suicide, use your creative imagination to create images contrary to such suggestions. The more positive imagery you create, the weaker the subconscious attacks become, and eventually the positive ones totally disassemble the negative recordings.[1]

There are people who punish themselves day and night because of their past mistakes. They must realize that on the path of Infinity they will have continuous opportunities to be more harmless, noble, and pure, and that no one can be wise without making mistakes and having defeats and humiliations in his past.

---

1. For exercises and visualizations, please refer to *New Dimensions in Healing* and *Joy and Healing*.

The defeat of one life prepares your victory for the future. On every step of your evolution, you create causes and you learn the laws controlling the effects. One day, all that you thought was wrong will be proven right by the analysis of karma. Nothing happens by accident. Things positive or negative create friction to cause you to enter the path of perfection. All will be forgiven in the ocean of Love because everything that has happened was to exhaust karma and prepare those causes that will help you climb toward new achievements.

The basic concept that you must develop is that you are essentially divine, and when that divinity is in the process of manifestation within you, no darkness can dwell in you. You are basically divine and perfect and pure. Impurity and imperfection are there for a period of time. Increase your innate divinity by manifesting Beauty, Goodness, Righteousness, Joy, Freedom, striving, and sacrificial service, and you will live in a pure light and forever remain in that purity.

You may ask, "Isn't self-punishment a good method to eradicate the causes in the subconscious mind?"

It may appear so. However, punishment creates one of the worst conditions during which additional recordings flow into the subconscious mind.

Every time you are punished or are punishing yourself, you are becoming unconscious. What is worse is that those elements that are in your conscious field, such as your ideas, thoughts, visions, expectations, regrets, etc., go in as posthypnotic suggestions during the period of your self-punishment.

After you punish yourself, you discover that you are in a more mixed-up condition than before. People will realize in the future that nothing can be accomplished by punishment. It is only education, enlightenment, and analysis that can work miracles.

All methods and forms of punishment are real crimes against the evolutionary current. Punishment solves momentary problems but plants long-range problems which require centuries to control, balance, and eradicate.

All those governments or nations that have been using the method of punishment on others are preparing destruction for themselves. This was the case in ancient Persia, Chaldea, Germany, and, recently, the Soviet Union.

16 | Advertisements

Most advertisements provide a source of manipulation of the subconscious mind. They create associative pictures or words to restimulate corresponding elements in your subconscious mind. Once these elements become active, you generally do not listen to the resistance of your logical mind.

This is how certain advertisements create greed in you, and you buy or accumulate things which you do not necessarily need. The gifts of Nature are then wasted, and money is accumulated in irresponsible hands.

Some of the advertisements are shown immediately after certain violent moments in the movie and when you are in a relatively hypnotic state. It is during such moments that the advertisements sink into your subconsciousness as strong posthypnotic suggestions.

There are also advertisements subliminally directed to your subconscious mind. These subliminal messages are imparted so fast that your conscious mind cannot catch them, nor can it filter them out. They go directly into your subconscious mind.

Subliminal messages are imparted during a moment of extreme happiness or sorrow, or in a moment when your analytical mind is intensely preoccupied with a problem or an object. Subliminal messages are given in various ways. One is by the use of recordings of verbal messages at an accelerated pace behind music or film tape. Another is by making drawings on top of other drawings or using photographs that the eye cannot detect but the subconscious mind can.

This is a blackout technique which, if developed a little more, will be the most frightening tool to control people and to exploit them in a number of ways.

Man cannot really detect such subliminal suggestions unless his Chalice is in the process of unfolding. If this is the case, he feels uncomfortable during any subliminal message broadcast in any form. Such a feeling may warn him not to listen to that music or watch that movie or look at certain advertisements.

It is also possible to detect subliminal suggestions through their results, provided that you have developed clear observation, are ready to see changes in your character or behavior, and can take action to destroy the roots of the cause in your subconscious mind.

17 | Suggestion

There is a difference between hypnotism and suggestion.

Suggestion does not mean to hypnotize people and plant commands in them that are posthypnotic.[1]

Suggestions are given while a man is totally awake. For example, you meet a friend and say, "You look healthy," or, "I feel you are going to be successful."

When a person highly respects you and trusts you, he believes in what you say. That belief acts as a healing agent in him and orients all his energies toward his well being. In this case you do not directly control him, but you allow him or encourage him to believe that he is healthy or that he will be successful. But he also may not

---

1. Please refer to *New Dimensions in Healing* for additional information on hypnotism.

believe you; he may even reject you. This is where suggestion differs from hypnotism.

In hypnotism you have no choice; you are going to act according to what the hypnotic command tells you while you are unconscious.

On the other hand, when you receive a suggestion, first, you are awake. Second, you have a choice to believe it or not. You are free to choose according to your karma.

Suggestions can turn into hypnotic commands when they are not done properly or if they are exaggerated.

If someone is really sick or in pain, your suggestions must be done very carefully. For example, if the medical conclusion is that the man will die soon, it is not proper to tell him that he is going to live another ten years. If he believes you, he will delay his death and suffer longer.

A suggestion is intuitively felt truth. You intuitively know that a person is going to live and be healed, and that person is convinced in his heart that he is going to be healed. The result is that because of your suggestion, a doubt is removed from his mind, a doubt created due to his affliction.

Suggestion is not given to change the course of events but to remove obstacles, doubts, suspicions that prevent a person from feeling his heart's Intuition.

Hypnotic commands are direct orders to be followed, even if the laws of Nature stand against them.

When M. M. speaks about suggestions, He definitely does not refer to the practice of hypnotism. Suggestions can have effects without putting the man to *sleep.*

Suggestions are applied in harmony with the principles and laws of Nature.

For example, I say to a person, "You have all the potentials to be a successful and influential man." This is a suggestion, and it is effective because in each man exist divine potentials which, if kindled, can lead the person to great success and make him influential.

In this case the suggestion is directed to the potentials of the man, trying to remove all that was hindering the actualization of the potentials.

Suggestions, if used with evil intentions, turn into hypnotic commands. For example, you say, "You look frail and sick. I feel that your end has come." Your suggestion turns into a hypnotic command because you dim his consciousness seventy to eighty percent by saying that.

In suggestions, your psychic energy helps the person to contact his Inner Reality. In a hypnotic command, the person is cut off from his consciousness and is enslaved.

Each right suggestion causes more awakening in a person. Each negative suggestion causes contraction in the consciousness and acts as a posthypnotic command.

In right or positive suggestions, you help make the person's soul cooperate and heal the condition.

In negative suggestion, your suggestion replaces the soul of the person. Every negative suggestion makes the soul withdraw if the person is not totally aware of the poison that is ready to be injected in him through negative suggestion.

It is possible that a negative suggestion may evoke a strong resistance in a man to reject it. Also, it is possible that his resistance and rejection become a main reason in his life to fight against the negative suggestion. Such a condition gradually turns into a plan in his mind to demonstrate throughout his life that the negative suggestion is not true and did not affect him.

18 | Forgiveness and the Subconscious Mind

Forgiveness does something very important. Forgiveness prevents things from going into the subconscious mind and sinking there. Before painful events become a part of the subconsciousness, forgiveness eliminates them.

That is why Christ said, "Before sunset, make peace with your enemies."

Forgiveness not only prevents a painful event from sinking into your subconscious mind, but it also prevents it from sinking into the subconscious mind of the one with whom you have a problem. This is a precious service which paves the way for better future friendships.

When people do not solve their problems before sleep, they take them into the Subtle World[1] and involve many people with their problems. Also, since they did not solve their problems before sleep, the problems sink into the subconscious mind. Like an iceberg, only the visible part of each problem stands in the conscious mind. This is also a problem because many other elements in the subconscious mind can come in contact with the conscious mind through the visible part of the iceberg. When you discover the problem and dissolve it, the iceberg comes to the surface and melts away. But if the problem is left for months, the iceberg increases in size and power.

There is a method that you can use so that eventually you get rid of the iceberg. Let us say that the iceberg is connected or related to a man who seems ugly and criminal to you. Using your creative imagination, you change the image of that man in a gradient scale to an image of a man whom you can respect, relate to, love, and even adore.

Your subconscious mind cannot guess what you are doing, and the ugly image changes in the subconscious mind which then accepts such a change and cooperates with you. When you are able to change the ugly image of the man into a grand image through your creative imagination, the corresponding ugly image dissolves.

First, you break the iceberg from the associating lines. Second, you bankrupt the ugly image in the subconscious mind and make the subconscious mind push the iceberg up to the conscious mind where it melts away in the heat of your positive reasoning and forgiveness.

---

1.   See also *Other Worlds*, Ch. 35, and *New Dimensions in Healing*, Ch. 44.

In another example, let us suppose that you have been afraid every night that someone will enter through the door and hurt you. This is an image in your subconscious mind. Try for a week to imagine yourself going to the door and finding an angel there instead of a thief. When you make this image strong enough, the computer of the subconscious mind will change the imagery and slowly dissolve it, and you will no longer fear that a thief will enter your room.

You can use this technique to eradicate those subconscious hindrances which prevent you from being successful, joyful, happy, healthy, and prosperous.

But whatever you create through your creative imagination, decide to use the result for the service of others. When you are using your creative imagination, always build images with the elements of Beauty, Goodness, Righteousness, Joy, Freedom, gratitude, and service. If your creative imagination is based on these elements, you will never build subconscious glamors.

Let us say that your husband (or wife) occasionally fights with you, and you do not take time to talk and clear it out. Time after time your subconscious recordings will grow, and gradually you will see that your husband becomes in your mind an uglier and uglier image. This will reach such proportions that you will try to get rid of him. Before you do that, with your creative imagination gradually improve his image to such a degree that you once again start loving him and respecting him. When you succeed in doing this, try to talk to him with love and try to create understanding between you. This will be difficult if the ugly image of your husband has grown in your mind for two to three years. The sooner you build an improved image of him, the better. You can use this technique with anyone who you think is hurting you. Your good thoughts alone will change him telepathically.

You can use your creative imagination also in the spirit of gratitude. For example you may think: he provides a good home for me, he is strong and handsome, he brings my food, he gave me a nice child, he protected me on several occasions, he was also great fun in the past, etc.

When such an image grows in your mind, it will go and attack the ugly image and disperse it and will prepare you for the opportunity for negotiation and understanding. As long as you maintain a state of hatred against each other, problems will remain unsolved.

Some people, instead of building beautiful images in their mind, do the contrary. They gossip, slander, and complicate the situation. Before you condemn and criticize, it will be helpful for you to discover why you are doing it. Most probably you are condemning, criticizing, and slandering people because you feel that it is the only way to feel secure, free, and pure.

Such a feeling is based on a wrong foundation because the more you criticize others, the more miserable you become; the more you condemn and slander others, the more fuel you add to your subconscious elements. Pouring all the trash into your subconscious mind will make you eventually realize that you are the one who is really the target of condemnation, criticism, and slander.

The quickest way to lose yourself is to attack others because of your subconscious commands.

19 | Observation

Observation is a real psychic power. The more you observe, the more spiritual you become, and a time comes when you distinctly see the existence of your not-self. You then become a Self, focused between your eyebrows, observing all that is going on in life.

It is in this state and position that you begin to live as a part of the All Self within all the phenomena of life.

The more you observe yourself, the more you see those things in your emotional and mental natures that do not serve a real purpose because they are not real or are not in harmony with the purpose of life.[1]

---

1. See *The Purpose of Life.*

When you become an observer, you become a cause instead of an effect.

Observation eventually makes you realize that you are the observer. There is also the object of observation and the mechanism that is used by the observer.

In average people's minds, these distinctions do not exist. Most of the time a person does not observe an object because he is identified with it. As long as one is identified with his own mechanism or with the object of observation, he does not exist by himself.

The objective of the Ageless Wisdom is to make us discover ourselves and see the difference between the Self, the object, and the mechanism of observation.

Once you learn to observe, you enter the road to freedom. Satisfaction makes you a slave; observation leads you to freedom.

Immediately as you observe the functions of the subconscious mind, you can control it. But if you do not observe it, it controls you.

Most of our habits are the result of identification. Identification is the result of a posthypnotic suggestion.

As long as you know how to observe, no one can hypnotize you; you remain awake.

Observation eventually leads you to the actualization of your True Self. In every recording of the subconscious mind are three elements — physical, emotional, and mental. If someone slaps your face, it is physical, emotions are involved, and also thoughts are involved.

If you get rid of one of them, the whole chain breaks and you can eliminate the recording. Remember that the subconscious mind has no logic, no discrimination, and everything there is equal to everything else. It is your conscious mind that must discriminate and know how to benefit from the condition of the subconscious mind.

To learn to observe yourself, you must observe someone who is acting under the pressure of the subconscious mind. When you have firsthand experience, then you can observe yourself and discover the moments when you are acting under the subconscious mind.

The subconscious mind has no discrimination. Any chain of events is built of many links. Links do not differ in the subconscious mind.

Suppose you fall down and break your fingers. During that time, someone dressed in white asked you, "Why didn't you watch your step?" There was also a radio playing in a car, and on a bush a bird was singing. These all form a chain with your fingers and the pain. If you see or hear any of the links of the chain, you will feel the same anxiety and pain that you had at the time of the accident, unless you were really conscious during it. For the subconscious mind, each link is equal to the other links, and each and all of them mean one thing: pain. Each link is a push-button to pain.

Suppose a girl asks a neighbor to go with her to a dance party. The neighbor comes dressed in a blue jacket. She feels uncomfortable and she turns to him and says, "Oh, I expected you to come a little early. You are always late."

Gradually her voice changes, and she becomes more serious. She continues, "I don't feel like going today. I don't know. You are not dressed well."

Eventually she fabricates another reason not to go to the dance party. But if she were to ask a Teacher, he would say, "Do you remember fifteen years ago when a man wearing the same kind of jacket tried to kidnap you?

Fortunately you escaped. But, you were wounded and scared to death." Her subconscious mind alarmed her because her neighbor was dressed in the same way as the man fifteen years ago. Thus, the subconscious mind cannot discriminate that this is not the same man, since he wears the same color jacket.

One of the highest achievements of human beings is to be able to stay awake and conscious and slowly to annihilate the control of the subconscious mind.

This is done by learning how to observe; how to detach yourself from the object of your observation; how to stay at the center between your eyebrows and remain focused there in your consciousness.

This is a major exercise on the spiritual Path. Nothing else can contribute to your growth if this foundation is not there. Learn how to concentrate mentally, emotionally, and physically. Learn how to meditate and how to observe.[2]

Especially observe your actions, emotions, and thoughts. Try to see how your subconscious mind operates. Have a set time daily to think about your observations. Try to see how the subconscious mind is working in the world and what are the consequences. Your efficiency in life and in your field of service will increase into many other fields as you become a more conscious person.

Try to observe also your conscious actions, and see why you call them conscious actions. What is the difference between the actions of these two minds?

---

2.   See also *The Science of Meditation* and *The Psyche and Psychism.*

Try to discover the moment when you were not able to act consciously but instead acted subconsciously.

All life responds to you if you create a conscious mind in yourself.

20 | Decisions and Subconscious Elements

Decisions made in unconscious moments are strong posthypnotic suggestions. Be careful in making any important decisions when you are not 100% conscious because, once you have made the decision, you will be forced by your subconscious mind to obey and actualize your own decision.

For example, when you were really angry and in fear, you said, "I am going to leave you" or "I am going to kill you."

Months or even years pass, but if such a decision in your subconsciousness is restimulated, you feel the tendency to leave or to kill. And when the stimulation reaches its highest degree, you have no choice but to obey your decision.

In olden days, certain tribes knew this fact. They used to make their enemies really angry so that the enemies made unreasonable and illogical decisions. Then it was easier to conquer them.

Once you lose your sanity in difficult conditions, not only do you hypnotize yourself, but you also take wrong actions. No right action is possible under conditions in which you are not 100% awake.

The astral plane and the subconscious mind must be bypassed if we want to make healthy decisions, ones that for a long time will be a source of happiness, success, prosperity, and expansion of consciousness.

Most of the decisions people make are forced on them by their fear, anger, hatred, and self-interest. These elements are mostly related to the subconscious mind and the lower astral plane.

Decisions must be the conclusions of the mind plus the Intuition.

The mind must base its conclusions upon

— real conditions

— past events

— present forces and energies

— the needs of the time

— the level of consciousness of the people related to its decision

The Intuition will see the decision in the long-range plan, in the light of higher events and available energies.

Decisions are the moving and directing sources of history, the life of the planet as a whole.

Most of the pain, suffering, and destruction are the result of wrong decisions, decisions not based on co-measurement.[1]

Co-measurement can only be achieved through the intuitive light because the Intuition synthesizes elements of the past, present, and future and gives a solution that fits your level and the time in which you exist.

As in many phenomena, there is also a critical point in the process of human evolution. This critical point becomes the boiling point when the past fights against concepts related to future transformation.

This critical point is often so strong that many souls become lost and cannot stand in the whirlpools of inner conflict. Ego, vanity, selfishness, separatism, and greed exercise a tremendous pressure upon the victim, and, in the meantime, his soul cries out for help from his vision.

The most decisive factor in this conflict is a person's karma. Those who have lived a life of selfless service, pure motives, inclusive love, and purity of mind have accumulated a good result in their karma and can usually cross the other shore in a relatively easy way. But those who were involved in selfish, manipulative activities with greed, slander, and self-interest fall into the tides of the bad results of karma and disappear. The Teaching says that pain and suffering follow their steps to prepare them for another chance in future lives.

---

1. See also *The Flame of Beauty, Culture, Love, Joy*, Ch. 4, and *A Commentary on Psychic Energy*, Ch. 7, on co-measurement.

When such crises come into our life, we must firmly establish ourselves in our faith and principles. We must get closer to our Teacher and ask for his direction based on his wisdom and experience.

There are two most critical points while the human soul is in the birth process. The first one is the moment when all is ready for the birth in the cave of the brain as a new human soul. The next is the point when the developing human soul begins to cross into the higher mind and tries to locate himself within the Spiritual Triad.

The subconscious mind expresses itself through your decisions in many other ways. One of them is through dreams in which people whom you hurt in secret come to your dream in various ways and frighten you or punish you.

Such dreams are formed by all the imaginations, feelings, and thoughts that your subconscious mind recorded during the secret and harmful acts that you committed on others.

During such acts, your worries about their possible revenge or their negative attitudes grow through a process of dramatization until they are mature and ready to haunt you.

It is clear that we punish ourselves with our harmful actions, words, feelings, decisions, and thoughts even if the victim does not react or organize against us.

Such dramatizations come to the surface as dreams when through some associations they are energized and called forth.

Of course they spread fear in our conscious mind if the conscious mind does not understand the process. Often through such fears the conscious mind takes further action or has various attitudes toward those whom the person hurt. Such actions and attitudes restimulate the subconscious contents further and add to the dramatization process, heavily complicating the conscious mind.

If the process is not understood and dissolved, it leads to mental deficiency and nervous complications and eventually to various sicknesses.

This is such a complicated process that the best cure is to live a harmless life. The more harmless you are, the fewer the possibilities for self-punishment.

Another method to cure the situation is to increase your service and help those whom you hurt, regardless of their attitudes and feelings against you.

The Ageless Wisdom says hatred cannot be cured by hatred. Hatred can be cured by love.

Worry is another conditioning factor that releases the subconscious elements or gathers more elements into it. The origin of worry can be physical or health conditions, attacking thoughtforms of malicious people who hate you, or it can be a thoughtform occupied by an entity attacking you on a particular occasion. Strive to free yourself from the subconscious mind so that you can make pure decisions as a human soul.

21 | The Concrete Mind

Some thoughtforms neither go to the Chalice nor into the subconscious mind but stay in the memory diskettes in the concrete mind. They cause many interferences which result in trouble for our thinking process.

For example, if we do wrong things at various times and occasions, they accumulate and interfere with our thinking. If we want to do something better, these impressions sneak in and say, "You always did wrong in the past, and you are going to do it again." This eventually leads us to continuous failures, and once we fall into irritation, anger, or fear, these failures go into our subconscious mind.

How can such a danger be avoided? There is a very easy method. After you make a mistake, try to correct it if you can.

If it is too late to correct it, do the following exercise:

1. Sit comfortably and close your eyes.

2. Visualize the event.

3. Take the perfect and correct action instead of the wrong one.

4. Repeat the visualization of the perfect event in detail, making it very real.

Such an exercise prevents failure images from accumulating in your mental sphere. Also, it defeats failure images and strengthens your spirit of striving toward perfection.

You can do such an exercise every day to prevent accumulations of failure images. If you do anything that makes you feel that it was not beautiful, not good, not righteous, etc., you can repeat the deed in your visualization, changing it to positive and successful action.

For example, if you cursed someone and felt bad in doing it, visualize yourself blessing him and feeling very happy. The sooner you try to eliminate the negative images or recordings, the better will be the condition of your thinking.

Our progress is not measured by time. We are not advised to hurry in our evolution because of time factors, making artificial efforts to be somebody. Rather, we must let Nature help us carry our responsibilities by clearing the obstacles we have in our mind.

22 | Guilt Feelings and the Subconscious Mind

Those who violate the Law of Conscience, the Law of Love, and civil laws develop a deep seated guilt complex which, because of fear, anxiety, and shame, goes into the subconscious mind and gradually controls the person's thinking, talking, and other actions. It is mostly a self-destructive recording which slowly dominates the person's waking hours as well as his dreams.

Certain negative imaginations also contribute to this recording of guilt. Certain people's gossip, slander, malice, and feelings of revenge build an especially horrible self-image for the person. Usually such people quit striving, quit their creative work and service, and become preoccupied with their guilt.

Self-punishment, which sometimes expresses in an act of confession, is one of the methods to be released from such a guilt. The church formulated the process of Confession which often helps people start a new creative cycle.

Some people are often terrified by their guilt to such a degree that they really want to be punished by the authorities, or they head toward suicide. Such methods and attitudes do not bring a satisfactory release, and every time their guilt is restimulated, it hits them and causes additional and various disturbances in their life.

There are some methods by which help can be brought to such people. For example, one of the methods is for them to compensate those whom they hurt. If the victims are not available, the guilty must help and serve other people as if they were doing it for their victims.

Second, they must see if they are really guilty, or if their guilt is a reflection of other people's opinions.

Third, they must consider whether it was karmic. Some of our harmful actions are purely karmic. They are retributive actions about which no one can do anything. Nature pays back; cause and effect do their job.

Fourth, was their action imposed by circumstances and people?

Fifth, was their action done to save others or with no bad motive?

Sixth, were they swayed by the currents of strong emotional energy or fears, or were they even to a certain degree unconscious?

Seventh, was their action the result of an eruption of the subconscious mind, or a result of a posthypnotic suggestion?

Analyzing these seven points may bring a certain release. You can also do some esoteric work to free yourself from such guilt attacks:

1. Solemnly promise yourself that with the help of God you will never fall into a similar guilty action.

2. For at least three months, pray and ask higher forces to strengthen, purify, and transform your mind.

3. Build a positive, beautiful image of yourself, making it more noble in every way. This must continue for six months.

4. Stand in the light of Christ and see yourself totally transformed.

5. Start helping those who are suffering under guilt and a bad self-image.

6. Ask for the assistance of your Guardian Angel to illuminate your mind and destroy the glamor of fear.

7. Develop virtues[1] that are the opposites of your vices.

---

1. For information on virtues, please see *The Psyche and Psychism* and *The Flame of the Heart*.

These seven points are very helpful, and they can save your life if you regularly engage yourself in the labor of self-transformation.

After you have some control over your emotions, it is good to remember your ugly or harmful actions and re-create them in such a way that they become the most noble actions. For example, if you stole some money and went through associated feelings, imagine the day and the moment of your act — but now act totally in the opposite way. Instead of stealing, give money. In your imagination help those whom you hurt. Spend your money to make the lives of those whom you hurt happy.

Building an opposing, positive image gradually destroys the ugly, negative image in your subconscious mind and brings you release.

23 | The Voice and the Subconscious

If you learn how to observe, often you will see that your voice and the voices of others change when they are under subconscious attacks. You see that the voice is tinged with fear, anxiety, jealousy, envy, hatred, malice, secrecy, etc.

At other times you see there is joy in the voice. There is freedom, hope, power, courage, future.

The subconscious mind exercises a tremendous power over our voice, and by observing the quality of our voice, we can see if we are "channeling" our subconscious mind.

If you develop your power of observation, you will handle people according to their level of consciousness. For example, if it is a subconscious promise, do not trust it. If it is a subconscious love, forget it. If it is a subconscious attack, be careful of it. The voice says things that cannot be seen in the words, so one must develop sensitive observation in hearing.

It is possible that a person has a great wealth of achievements but cannot share them with others or use them for his own benefit because of his voice and manners. This occurs when the person makes every kind of effort to improve his inner man, but his subconscious mind and the outer example in his environment, especially in childhood, enslave him and impose upon him a special tone of voice, a way of speech and manners. It is here that such a person needs help. And the help is to change the voice and manners and bring them into line with his achievements.

I remember a high level minister whose voice was like the voice of a chicken. He used to say wonderful things, but without deep affect. When I gave him special exercises so his voice would reflect his own level, he became the most influential minister.

Artificial exercises to change our voice create various psychological problems. The real help is not to make people change their voice but their level of consciousness and clean their subconscious mind. If these two are not done, a person can change his pitch but not his tonality. Tonality holds the secret, and it is the one that affects people and affects the cells and atoms of their bodies.

Spiritually advancing people change their voices and tonality, but this comes naturally. With such a change, their magnetism and their power of influence over other people is also changed.

A voice that is the expression of jealousy, revenge, vanity, or ego always sounds the same and hurts people's consciousness, even if he or she talks about joyful things. The subconscious mind dominates the tonality of the voice.

Success comes when the inner orientation, motives, and visions change.

A lady could not find a nice man to marry. Every time she met a man, she was deeply disappointed. One day she spoke to me about her problem. I suggested that she read from the Teaching and do certain meditations. Eight months passed and one day she introduced me to her boyfriend, a handsome gentleman, the one she was waiting for. Her voice in these eight months had gradually changed.

The voice not only subjectively affects people, but it also increases the magnetism of the person as he expands his consciousness and slowly frees himself from the domination of his subconscious mind.

The best way to change the voice is to unfold the petals of the Chalice, purify the subconscious mind, and grow as a soul. Sometimes the growth of the soul occurs in moments of sacrificial and heroic services done with great joy and in the spirit of gratitude.

One can slowly see that

- There is the voice of the bodies

- There is the noise of the bodies

- There is the voice of the personality, positive or negative

- There is the voice of the Solar Angel[1]

- There is the voice of the human soul, the Spiritual Triad, and the Self

- There is the voice of your Master

- There is the voice of the Ancient of Days

People often try with artificial methods to change a person's voice. It works for a while, but then it creates friction in the inner mechanisms because the tonality of the voice is equal to the sum total that the man is. To change a person's voice, one needs to raise the level of his consciousness and unfold his soul.

---

1.   See also *The Solar Angel*, *Other Worlds*, Ch. 59, "The Guardian Angel," and *New Dimensions in Healing*, Ch. 30, "The Solar Angel."

24 | Chanting and the Subconscious Mind

Throughout the ages various religious and philosophical organizations taught their followers to chant certain mantrams, prayers, or affirmations for their physical well-being, for their emotional peace, for their enlightenment, or for their spiritual achievements. Still today, many religions have their words of power, mantrams, invocations, affirmations, prayers which they repeat twenty-one times, forty times, seventy times, one-hundred-five times, and sometimes for hours and days.

When something is repeated mechanically, it loses its power and sinks into the subconscious mind. There it turns into a posthypnotic suggestion or into an urge or a drive, and, gaining control day after day from this mechanical repetition, the accumulated hypnotic suggestions increase in power and begin to control the mind. For a short while, these accumulations urge the conscious mind to work hard to provide for the demands of the subconscious mind.

Very often it happens that the conscious mind cannot follow the demands of the subconscious mind, and it pushes these demands or drives back to the subconscious mind which in its turn bounces them back into the conscious mind with more power.

If this continues for a while, confusion sets in in the conscious mind. In unexpected moments, the actions of the conscious mind are intensified by the force of the subconscious currents with much disturbance. The person appears to be absent-minded, forgets things, looks at things but cannot see, hears things but does not grasp, decides to do something but suddenly changes his direction. The person feels irritation when the subconscious mind forces it again and again, and the conscious mind sends the message back to the subconscious mind as an irrational demand.

Those who use mantrams, etc., mechanically for three to seven years show serious mental problems.

But how should we pray, repeat our mantrams or invocations, or even our affirmations? The answer is in a conscious state of mind, understanding and realizing the words that we are repeating again and again. There is nothing wrong in repetition unless it is done mechanically.

During mechanical repetition or chanting, the invocation, mantram, affirmation, or prayer does not go into the subconscious mind in its purity, but it mixes with the thoughts that we allow to come into our consciousness.

These thoughts may appear not to have any relation to the mantram, but they are still evoked at some point in the mantram, or by the mood or condition of our physical, astral, or mental body. Definitely they associate with the mantram and sink into the subconscious mind.

Sometimes these associations are not so dangerous, but sometimes they are. For example, suppose I am chanting, "*I love all human beings*," and in the meantime my mind remembers a traitor who gave me great anxiety and grief. Now these sensations and his image will associate with each other and sink into my subconscious mind.

Every time I repeat my affirmation, the whole experience with the traitor will be restimulated, and the **key** of the restimulation will be "*I love all human beings.*"

If during my chanting I accumulate various other associations, you can imagine what chaos I will create in my subconscious mind. This is why we must chant a mantram with **concentration** — as if nothing else exists around us. We must chant it rhythmically. Concentrated rhythm is a power, the secret of which is known only to Great Ones Who use mantrams to switch mighty energies off and on.

A very powerful result is obtained by concentration, by conscious chanting, and by the rhythm of chanting. There is great power in repetition if it is done consciously. Every time you become mechanical, your words go into the subconscious mind and sink there, and they eventually find some affinities with other elements, turn into "a soup," and into an incoherent and confused demand upon the conscious mind.

But if repetition or chanting is done consciously, it affects the heart center, the head center, and the Mental

Permanent Atom which broadcast the message to Higher Worlds.

The first response comes from your Intuitional Plane, which enlightens you about what to do to actualize your desires, demands, or wishes. Second, your demand goes and hits the Spiritual Triad and your Solar Angel.

The Spiritual Triad is formed by two advanced Beings, Who, along with your Solar Angel, form a Trinity. This is what we call the higher sphere of *Superconsciousness*. When your invocation penetrates into this sphere, you feel that your wishes are on the path of actualization.

For example, all the demands of Jesus were fulfilled because He knew how to ask. And because He was in contact with Higher Worlds, His demands were immediately met. He said, *"Ask, and you shall receive,"* but most of us do not know how to ask because asking requires a conscious and focused mind. If there are subconscious currents in our mind, or blackouts, or confusion, or lack of faith, the demand is not recorded and answered.

We know how much we pray to be led "from darkness to light, from the unreal to the real, from death to immortality, from chaos to beauty" — but we see that, instead, we are occupied with darkness, with the unreal, with death, and with chaos. For this reason we do not see our prayers or mantrams answered.

The result becomes discouraging, and because our mechanical prayers are not answered, we conclude that prayers, mantrams, affirmations, and invocations are totally useless. We then turn our face from the spiritual realm to matter, to the politics of exploitation and manipulation.

Once you learn to be focused and conscious at the moment of your prayers or invocations, you receive your answer. *"Ask and you shall receive,"* said the Great Lord.

You must ask again and again with an alert and conscious attitude of mind, until the atoms of your body, emotions, and mind are strongly impressed. It is this impression that will put into motion your Superconscious Mind where Great Entities, in Their turn, will pass your demand to the Higher Worlds.

Asking with a conscious mind is also a method which eventually builds the bridge between your conscious mind and Superconscious Mind. When this is done, the *Unconscious,* which is now beyond the Superconscious Mind, will send you periodic flashes.

When you recite mantrams, even in a foreign language such as Sanskrit, Latin, or Ancient Armenian, the superconscious levels reveal the meaning, unfolding the mantram layer after layer until all becomes clear to you.

For example, if you are reciting *"Avira virma yeti,"* which means *"O Self-revealing One, reveal Thyself in me,"* you understand it to a certain degree in your waking consciousness, but if you chant it in the superconscious levels, it unfolds like fireworks, each spark in its turn expanding into another burst of fire. The activities of the revealing Self appear in all seeds, in all forms, in all systems and galaxies — and, in the meantime, you feel as if you are *That Self.* When you come down to the level of common consciousness, you feel as if you had been enjoying a great spiritual feast, which is just over, but you still feel the regenerating effects of it and the rising flow of aspiration that grows within you.

Some reach such a high level in superconscious realms through meditation and contemplation, others in building the Golden Bridge, others as a grace encouraged by their karma.

Disciples can reach such a level by deliberately withdrawing themselves into the superconscious realms.

The mantrams chanted in the superconscious realms are *words in silence.* It is in silence that your words become audible to Higher Beings. Or it is in silence or in a vacuum that your demand reaches its destination without meeting any hindrances.

Teachers advise us to practice regular meditation so that eventually we learn how to penetrate into the super-conscious realms of Light.

Christ revealed a mystery when He said, *"When you pray, go into your inner room, and after shutting your door, pray to your Father Who is in secret."*[1]

The "inner room" or private room, is the Superconsciousness. To "shut the door," means to withdraw yourself from your fourth mental plane and detach yourself from your emotional and physical bodies and enter into a higher plane, according to your present evolution. It is in such a state of beingness that one must pray and the Father will answer you. The Father is not answering you because of your needs, since He already knows your needs even if you are not in the "inner room." He is answering you because in the "inner room" you are in one moment becoming Him. This is the secret. Knowing your needs, you answer them yourself. You can answer your needs only when you know your needs when you are in the "inner room." Your Father is secretly in you, hidden in you, and He is revealed to you only in the "inner room."

---

1.   Matt. 6:6

The "inner room" is that state of consciousness in which you unite with the Father within you Who was previously hidden from you.

In Asia, I had a Teacher who used to sit for hours near the rivers or lakes or under trees and chant. One of his mantrams was the word "beauty."

Once I asked him to explain to me what he was doing. He told me that he sits in a very comfortable position, kneeling or cross-legged, withdraws his consciousness from the world and from his body, emotions, and mind, and starts repeating the word "beauty," every time trying to penetrate into deeper layers of that concept. He said, "In each sitting I find a deeper meaning, have a deeper revelation, and, curiously enough, afterward I feel happy, healthy, inspired, and energetic."

I knew him for five years. He always had a magnificent smile on his face and was profoundly joyful, serene, and healthy. When I left him, he was ninety-seven years old but could ride a horse and swim for hours.

One must reach such a state of consciousness to be able to experience an expanding revelation in each chanting.

Once I asked him if he did not exhaust the word "beauty." He gave me a big smile and said, "Beauty is the Cause of every form. How can one exhaust it? It is a key in my consciousness by which I open many doors into higher realms."

I have seen him examining a flower with deep admiration. Once when there was a great thunderstorm, he acted like a child, looking at the lightning and screaming and jumping, repeating, "Beautiful, beautiful, beautiful! Oh, how beautiful! My Lord, what a beauty!"

Every word is a form. The archetype of it is rooted in the Great Mystery of the Universe. It is possible to contact such a mystery by chanting in the secret room of your superconscious realms.

Some mantrams are the names of entities. Using these names over and over again can also create problems and force them to act under our willpower, which may create drastic reactions.

Mantrams — words of power — eventually turn into the bodies of certain forces, if they are not the names of entities, devas, or angels.

Thus, before using a mantram you need protection and a scientific knowledge of how to use it to avoid creating problems and upsetting all the realms of your subconscious mind.

Until we know exactly how to use the mantram scientifically, consciously, and with readiness, we must follow the method of meditation and sacrificial service to expand our consciousness and come in conscious contact with those who will reveal to us the secret of the use of the mantram.

Some mantrams fulfil your wishes in a short time. Some of them bring much energy into your system, but all these work against your interest and mental health if you are not ready to receive the gifts or energies drawn to yourself.

The consciousness of some people is far ahead of all that they have in their mental equipment due to their past conscious achievements.

Some people have advanced beingness because of their purity. They can even perform miracles because they do not have in their nature hindrances to the incoming energies.

What we need is to expand our consciousness and create a corresponding beingness and a purified, disciplined, and synthesized mental body.

All our achievements must be gained by our conscious labor.

Some people can perform "miracles" under hypnotic suggestion or because some entity has possessed them. These are not signs of expansion of consciousness or development of beingness.

The harmonious development of a person involves all his vehicles, which have to be developed with his conscious labor.

The more we cleanse our subconsciousness, the purer becomes our consciousness, which in turn opens to us the doors to higher levels of consciousness.

25 | Prayer and Subconsciousness

We must learn to remain conscious during our prayers and invocations to avoid filling our subconscious mind with various hypnotic suggestions.

When you say a prayer mechanically, you activate your subconscious mind and the subconscious mind absorbs your prayer as a posthypnotic suggestion. Sometimes as you are doing some work, you feel that your mind is telling you something else such as repeating a song, repeating a mantram, or repeating a word which eventually causes disturbances in your mental body. But if you consciously say the prayer, being totally concentrated and focused in what you are saying, you impress your four lower ethers and the heart, throat, and head centers which take the message to the Chalice. From the Chalice it is raised to the three entities that are part of your Spiritual Triad.[1] These entities then respond to your prayer. If you are doing something unconsciously, unwillingly, without purpose and goalfitness, you have very little effect. But if you are putting all your power, energy, heart, and spirit into what you are doing, the response and the effect is much more than you expect.

We must not fall into mechanicalness. We must pray consciously and earnestly so that these three entities, who always see the face of "the Father," bring our wishes back to us and actualize our visions. Failure to pray consciously and earnestly makes people stay as they are. For example, we say "Lead us, O Lord, from darkness to Light," but we do not work for light. We cannot even see the difference between darkness and light, between dark actions and light actions, dark emotions and light emotions, dark thoughts and light thoughts. And we do not see any progress, any improvement in our life because there is no answer. We go to the door of our Father and do not knock, then come back and say, "Father is not answering."

Go knock on the door and say, "I want wisdom." Father will give it to you. That is what Christ said.

There was a lady who went to a judge and said, "Please take care of my problem." He said, "Lady, get lost." She returned the next day and said, "Please." He said, "If you come again, look at what I will do to you." And she still came back, and the judge was angry with her persistence but finally said, "Come, come in. What is your

---

1. Note: These entities are the Devas of the three permanent atoms which form the Spiritual Triad — Mental Permanent Atom, Intuitional Permanent Atom, Atmic Permanent Atom.

problem? Okay, let us solve it." Christ said you must do it just the same way. You must consciously go within yourself, find the Source from which you are expecting your answer, and ask from It.

A prayer repeated unconsciously can settle itself in the subconscious mind as a strong posthypnotic suggestion. For a while, it becomes a source of energy for us, pushing us toward achieving good results from it. But very soon we notice that the bodies are not ready to be constantly charged with that posthypnotic suggestion. They show signs of exhaustion and act abnormally because of the constant pressure of the posthypnotic suggestion.

Even "good" posthypnotic suggestions create a very disturbed state of mind if the suggestions are not welcomed by the readiness of the vehicles. Another factor is that you may have "positive" suggestions and your bodies may be ready, but your normal consciousness has no information about what is going on behind the posthypnotic suggestion and your vehicles. Your consciousness may not accept what is going on between the subconscious mind and your vehicles without its agreement.

Such a condition can create further complication in the whole etheric, emotional, and mental mechanism.

The solution is to increase our conscious moments and never do things *unconsciously*.

Consciousness includes

1. Our experiences and sensations of physical objects

2. Feelings — generated both by contact with objects and with inner emotions and images

3. Thinking experiences, imagination, visualizations, daydreaming, reasoning, logic, decision, discrimination, comparison, and so on

4. Intuitive experiences and foresight, insight, premonition, and the like

5. Experiences of determination and will, both in relation to outer objects and events, and inner objects and events related to the four above points

But, because of our identification with various outer and inner elements, we remain unconscious or semiconscious and tend to become the process instead of the observer.

If we keep ourselves conscious every moment and become aware of these five forms of experience, we will discover our True Self and life will become an endless series of instructions and the cause of supreme enlightenment.

Prayer is related to these five states of consciousness.

Conscious prayer is not only a contact with higher levels but also an experience of identification with them.

In the prayer, we open ourselves to higher energies and fuse with them.

The ultimate goal of prayers is fusion with the Source toward which we aim our *prayers*.

26 | Sex and the Subconscious

One of the strongest and blindest urges in the subconscious mind is the sex urge. You can find in the subconscious storage not only the records of your sex life from the past but also the accumulated images from your present life. All the sexual activities you saw in your childhood, the stories, the pornographic magazines, movies, your wild imaginations and dreams — all are there.

Most of these recordings are responsible for the kind of relationships we have with others. They are responsible for our marriages and, in a high percentage, for our divorces and the pain and suffering that we go through in our sexual life.

These sex recordings are very inflammable, sensitive, easily impressed images which control our life from birth to death. Social pressure, law, tradition, and religion cannot really control these urges which, once inflamed, destroy all restrictions and, like a flood, go to their destruction.

At the present there are also energies that are released from higher sources related to our creative centers. One of them is the Seventh Ray which causes tremendous stimulation in our subconscious mind and our sacral center. Sometimes such stimulations are so strong that a person becomes a victim and tries to satisfy his sexual urges beyond his normal limits.

These powerful energies released in Space can work through our subconscious mind and bring us unending problems, or they can be caught consciously within our higher creative centers and used to further the Plan of the transformation of the entire life on the planet.

Here again we come to the discipline of meditation, readiness, and purity in order to avoid being drawn within the tides of the released energies.

Some people cannot record and accumulate these energies consciously, so the energies go and fill their subconscious realms. But, with the help of a Teacher, we can eventually stop energies from going to the subconscious mind and instead use them in a creative labor.

Again, the cure for the overstimulation in which all the world is involved is not to increase laws and punishment but to

— Find a method of sublimation

— Reduce the sources of overstimulation

— Increase the number of thoughtforms related to the ultimate purpose of sex, to the beauty of the sexual relationship, and to its spiritual significance[1]

Once these three steps are scientifically put into effect, our subconscious volcano will slowly relax and become dormant.

Most of the sex we are involved in is under the pressure of our subconscious mind. We are victims of the things that we have seen, heard, and read which we have collected in our subconscious mind.

It is observed that during the sexual act our consciousness is 60% to 70% in a hypnotic condition. Care must be taken that during such periods people do not plant hypnotic suggestions in each other's minds.

The sex images existing in the subconscious mind have a powerful influence over us, and we must try to get rid of them as soon as we can before we pass away.

Some people feel that they can conquer their sex urge if they waste it carelessly by changing their partners and falling into sexual license. They think that in this way the pressure of the urge can be exhausted.

It is true that after such "freedom" people may act a little more conservatively. In reality, what has happened is that they have hurt their sexual organs and destroyed their own vitality, but the sexual urge remains alive, although they cannot satisfy it.

---

1. See also *Sex, Family, and the Woman in Society* and *Woman, Torch of the Future.*

When some people feel sick, hurt, or suffer under various circumstances, they lose the sex urge and think that they have overcome their subconscious sex urge. This is not a victory over the sex urge. Control over the sex urge must come through burning the thoughtforms accumulated in the subconscious mind.

Others think that when they fast or submit themselves to religious asceticism, they can get rid of the sex urge. It is observed that such kinds of efforts are superficial. The only way to conquer the subconscious sex urge is to follow the three steps given above. Even with these steps, it takes time since we have increased our karma with sex violations or sexual waste. But once we conquer, we see the beauty of sex and the happiness that life gives us.

It is wonderful to discover who is driving the car of our life. Is it us, or some other force accumulating within our subconscious mind?

People ask how sublimation occurs. First of all, sublimation of the sex energy cannot occur if the subconscious mind is full of sex and lust images. These must be cleaned out before sublimation takes place. Thus the person must have enough experience in meditation and visualization to raise the forces of the lower centers to higher centers.

It is through meditation and visualization that the energies of the sacral center are lifted to the throat center.

Some people think that sublimation occurs if they fast sexually. This does not sublimate, but it takes the heat away for a while. Sexual heat manifests mostly through a wild imagination.

Real fasting must be carried on mentally as well as emotionally and physically, accompanied by meditation and visualization.

The focus of our consciousness is mostly within the lower centers. Until this focus is moved up to the throat and heart centers, persistent control cannot be gained over the sex force.

To sublimate our sex force, we need to do the following:

— Avoid feeding our subconscious mind

— Avoid restimulating its contents

— Practice threefold fasting — mental, emotional, and physical

— Use meditation and visualization to change the focus of our consciousness

— Engage in creative activities and heavy physical labor

— Use creative imagination to disintegrate ugly memories and forms related to sex

— Observe our conversations and try to become involved with ideas related to humanity

These steps will be very helpful to decrease the pressure from the subconscious mind and sublimate the sexual energies.

It is also possible to practice the following exercises to control excess sex energy or lust. Lust is the overflow of sex energy used to force sex on others, without exercising the slightest consideration or thinking about the consequences. In general, the force of a subconscious surge can be weakened if you change a link in the chain of the surge. Immediately when one of the links changes its form, the chain of the surge loses its power and its meaning.

The subconscious surge is formed by symbols or words in association which make a chain. It is the chain that must be weakened by disrupting or changing one of its links. In this way, the pattern itself is disrupted.

Lust can be burned away by doing these exercises.

The First Exercise

This exercise can be done by two people, one acting as the director, the other as the doer.

- Visualize situations that overstimulated your sexual urge. Choose ten memories.

- Take the first one and in your visualization make the whole image burn with fire until it is annihilated.

- The director must guide the doer again and again until he is able to burn the whole image completely. This must be done gradually, step by step, encouraging the doer to follow the instructions to annihilate completely the image of lust.

- The time can be extended to one-half hour. Then rest must be given to the doer. The director can make him repeat each of the ten images several times until all the images are annihilated.

When the first exercise has been done at least ten times for one month, the next one must be done in the following manner.

The Second Exercise

- Close your eyes and relax. Try to visualize a scene of lust and slowly change the nature of the actors into flowers and stones and use them to build a garden.

- For example: The woman or man is engaged in lustful intercourse using alcohol and various other objects such as fruits, bottles, food items. Now change the woman into the most beautiful flower, the man into the most beautiful tree. Change the other items into various kinds of rocks. Now build a garden and plant the flower and tree. Help them grow and multiply, and then visualize every article becoming a flame. Then visualize heavy rains — and all is gone.

The Third Exercise

- See a red flame six inches away from your lower back. See the flame extending up to a location six inches behind your heart and there turning into a most beautiful flower with many colors and with the most precious fragrance.

- Visualize this flower slowly rising and turning into a halo above your head.

- When you visualize the halo, try to create a song in your mind and sing it. Or do a painting, or a dance, or create music, etc. Use any talent that you have for twenty-five minutes.

These exercises must be started with relaxation, continued with conscious visualization, and ended with remembering where you are and who the director is.

After the exercises, keep silent for not less than ten minutes.

It is probable that your lust will disappear after a short time. You can also use the form of these exercises to annihilate greed and other vices.

The period for each exercise is one month — not less than thirty minutes a day. Do them after getting the permission of your doctor.

Those who have certain vices or unacceptable social behaviors are mostly diagnosed as being the victims of their abnormal brain chemistry, etc. But the reality is that it is our consciousness and subconsciousness that create the mechanisms of our brain, glands, and chemistry.

People say that a person has a tumor in his brain or that a part of the brain is enlarged; that is why he is sexually overstimulated or does crazy things. But the truth is that the tumor is found in the brain *because* his sexual energies were misused and overused and *because* of his imagination, circumstances in life, experiences, examples, education, tradition, and prenatal urges and drives.

The subconscious and conscious minds actually control the chemistry of our bodies.

27 | Surge of the Subconscious Mind

The subconscious mind reacts under a law that can be called the *Law of the Pledge*. Many Teachers observe that this law operates every time a person makes a definite pledge to walk on the spiritual Path. What does this law do? This law opens the doors of your subconscious mind and lets some of the repressed elements come out to the surface of consciousness as strong urges and drives.

For example, certain urges and drives that you were able successfully to conceal in the subconscious mind come out and sometimes devastate your life. Urges related to sex, greed, vanity, separatism, jealousy, and other vices come to the surface and involve you in various humiliating activities.

Also, the Law of the Pledge makes you a catalyst that restimulates the subconsciousness of people around you, creating a complicated situation in your life. For example, not only do you act in a weird manner, but also the people around you do the same.

Your pledge also brings out virtues and treasures hidden in your Chalice.

The mixture of these various currents of forces in your daily life brings much confusion within you. One moment you are the most noble person, and another moment you act as a slave of your vices. Observing yourself in such situations, you may almost hate yourself. People who are close to you, seeing such changes in you, think you are a hypocrite.

The battle lasts long until your virtues increase in power and until you exhaust the subconscious urges and drives and bring out the trash floating in your subconscious mind.

The period of confusion and trial is shorter if you really press forward to actualize your pledge through your daily meditation, study, and service.

There is another thing that happens. Not only do negative elements within you fight against your decision to walk on the Path, but also those negative elements invite certain dark forces which, seeing that you are ready to enter the Path of Light, begin to fight against you according to the degree that your karma permits them to fight.

Every element in you that is against Beauty, Goodness, Righteousness, Joy, Freedom, striving, and service gives its permission or invitation to other negative elements to fight against you and complicate your life.

All these negative forces do not want you to follow the path of perfection but to be the slave of the chaotic forces in Nature.

Dark forces have various techniques — sometimes powerful, sometimes amusing. For example, they lead you into relationships which exhaust your time, energy, and money and do not give you a chance to follow your pledge. Or, they may help you open very profitable businesses that will ultimately work against your pledge. They can even lead you to books or groups that change the course of your life in a negative direction.

Against all these negative forces, you have the following:

1. Your pledge

2. The protection of your Solar Angel and Teacher

3. The fiery currents of your virtues

4. The prayers and good thoughts of your fellow travelers

5. The continuous, persistent striving toward the ideal you have in your mind

If you hold fast to all of these, you will see that any attack from whatever source will help your progress on the Path and increase your wisdom and energy.

Those people who really want to walk on the Path feel joy when they encounter difficulties and when the contents of the subconscious mind begin to surge out.

First, they think that it is good to learn how to confront difficulties and problems. Second, they want to meet all the elements hidden in their subconscious mind.

To clear the subconscious mind may take ages or many incarnations, but when a person makes his pledge, he wants to confront the surges as much as he can and pave his way toward Mastership.

Everyone who pledges to his Soul or Teacher to stay on the Path in spite of all difficulties also draws energy from the Hierarchy.

Those who are fearless make it, and one day they see that they do not enjoy a life without battle against opposite forces.

The subconscious mind has many layers, and it is the best policy to dig them out intelligently and annihilate them.

To control the currents of subconscious elements, you will use keen observation, nobility, and try to stay in your spiritual principles. You will be surprised to see how much ugliness will come out as thoughts, as imagination, as hypnotic suggestions. If you deal with them as an observer and do not become involved with them, you will eventually be victorious.

Make your pledge to stay on the path of Beauty, Goodness, Righteousness, Joy, Freedom, striving, and service, and if you fail, do not condemn yourself, do not give up, but see why you failed and start again — and again.

Many Teachers advise their disciples to be compassionate and tolerant toward fellow disciples who go through a hard time confronting the elements of their subconscious mind. If love, compassion, and tolerance are used toward a co-disciple who occasionally fails and demonstrates defective moral standards, most of his problems can be solved. The keys to use are loving understanding, or non-condemnation, and a readiness to help and uplift a brother who is driven away by the flood of the subconscious mind and attacked by dark ones.

It is possible that a failing brother can bring damage to the group of disciples, even to the Teaching, but all this is temporary. When the subconscious elements are exhausted or weakened, the brother will again search for the Path of Light and will walk on it full of experience and wisdom.

This is why when a brother errs the co-disciples send good and loving thoughts to him, keep him in the light, and never criticize him.

Among those who fail, there are also traitors and betrayers. Even against them compassion is used and strict silence.

This is why you need to find your Teacher and follow his advice, especially when you feel that you are losing your interest in the Path or becoming involved in shameful activities. Get closer to your Teacher, as a man who clings to a piece of wood when in danger of drowning.

Your Teacher will be extremely helpful in the days of darkness.

28 | Fear and the Subconscious Mind

Part I

Fear is an octopus in our subconscious mind. It relates almost every element in our subconscious mind to everything else. That is why the major restimulator and push-button in our mind is fear. Many people who sense negative and destructive forces know this very well. People who know this fact manipulate us by using their formula of fear. Once we are afraid, or once the fear penetrates into our subconscious mind, our subconscious mind begins its mobilization and releases the elements of hatred, anger, jealousy, revenge, treason, and associated imagery and imagination.

A man who is engulfed in fear will do almost anything someone wants him to do because fear shuts off the brain and logic and makes the person a slave.

Dark forces use fear to occupy and possess us. Some of our dreams and nightmares are the result of their projections which, associated with the fears in our subconscious mind, create horrors and paralysis in our life.[1]

The Tibetan Master, speaking about fear, gives certain formulas which He says can be used very effectively. One of them is a mantram which must be repeated daily many times with concentration, faith, and will power:

> *Let reality govern my every thought, and truth be the master of my life.*[2]

The second suggestion from the Tibetan Master is to do the following visualization exercise:

a. Still the physical body.

b. Quiet, by temporary inhibition, the astral body.

c. Link up with the Ego [Solar Angel] and definitely reason out the proper method of procedure in meeting the difficulty. Having exhausted all the higher rational methods, and clearly seen your course of action, you then —

---

1. For more information about fear, please see Ch. 104, *The Psyche and Psychism.*
2. Alice A. Bailey, *A Treatise on White Magic* (New York: Lucis Publishing Co., 1972), p. 239.

d. Raise your vibration as high as may be and call down from the intuitional levels added light on the situation. If your intuition and reasoning faculty in meeting produce harmony, then proceed, knowing as an occult fact past your altering — a law immovable — that nothing can happen but what is for the best. You are being guided and he who sees the end from the beginning makes no error.[3]

Such an exercise brings in the fiery current of light from the Intuitional Plane and burns away accumulations of fear not only in the subconscious mind but also, correspondingly, in the astral plane. It also burns the sediments of fear circulating in the blood stream.

There are, of course, sources of fear that only your Teacher or Master can fight against, and They often provide a shield for your protection.

In a monastery I once visited, the Teachers used to train their students in fearlessness. This was a six-month course through which only some of the students were able to go. It was a risky course, but the basic foundation was that nothing would happen to you if it were not in your karma. Of course, as students, we argued about such a belief, but the course was there, and those who had passed through it seemed to show a high level of leadership in their life.[4]

The course had twelve primary steps:

---

3. Alice A. Bailey, *The Beacon* (Sept./Oct. 1989): p.133.
4. See also *New Dimensions in Healing*, Ch. 63, "Healing Through Struggle."

1. To jump across a precipice, four to five meters wide

2. To swim through a very fast river to the other shore

3. To deliver messages in the dark through forests

4. To find a fellow student at night in the wilderness

5. To survive alone seven days in the forest or wilderness

6. To ride on bulls or wild horses

7. To follow dogs and wild cats at night

8. To sleep in a cabin without closing the doors

9. To show no fear when fires blaze

10. To enter into flaming houses and bring out certain objects

11. To stand guard on the walls of the monastery

12. To catch snakes with our hands

These exercises were called the mild course. The heavy course was given when a candidate for leadership passed at least six times through each exercise.

We had fifteen to twenty boys in the school who were called "daredevils." They had no fear in their eyes. Their presence used to inspire daring and courage. They used to do the most daring labors in great joy and with extreme tactfulness.

There were also exercises dealing with death and horror. These last, as graduation exercises, were very subjective and were related to astral phenomena and dark attacks.

The reason for these exercises was to make the person realize that he is a *Self* — and there is no power in the world that can defeat him.

Each victory or trial used to increase the students' joy. They were daredevils. The most obvious characteristic they had was a "divine carelessness," a "divine indifference." One day when I was asking my Teacher about their carelessness and indifference, he said, "These are the result of a realization and inner experience of immortality and an identification with the *Changeless* within them."

29 | Fear and the Subconscious Mind

Part II

As stated in the previous chapter, one of the inhabitants of the subconscious world is the octopus of fear. It grows, year after year, using the other inhabitants for its own nourishment and subjectively controls all actions of man on the physical, emotional, and mental planes.

To deal with the existing fears and gradually to annihilate them from our subconscious mind is the greatest service that we can render to ourselves and others.

Fear manifests through certain thoughtforms in our mental sphere and tries to control our life. It is important that we recognize these thoughtforms and handle them scientifically, as a thoughtform of fear contains many other vipers from our subconsciousness.

There are three kinds of thoughtforms. One is the thoughtform originated from an idea. Another is the formation of a thought about events or the formation of impressions coming from life in general. The other is a thoughtform built from contact with subconscious fears.

Thoughtforms that present ideas last for a long time and become a source of psychic energy in our activities. They uplift the level of our relation to the world and human beings and slowly transform our consciousness.

Most thoughtforms built around painful emotions sink into the subconscious mind. A part of this thoughtform flashes to the surface of the mind as a memory, but its roots are in the subconscious mind. Such events, which are filled mostly with fear and terror, when restimulated draw the chain of terror and fear from the subconscious mind, creating real disturbances in our waking consciousness.

Thoughtforms woven around painful life events and thoughtforms linked with the subconscious mind are, in general, called negative thoughtforms. Everyone of us must try to free ourselves from these thoughtforms if we want to have a healthy, happy, intelligent, and successful life.

Thoughtforms fabricated by the subconscious mind built around events and impressions coming from life in general can be destroyed relatively easily if they are not part of the system of our principles, moral codes, and standards.

There are many laws that are effective in the mental plane. One of them can be formulated as follows: "Opposing thoughtforms in the mental plane annihilate each other." For example, if you think about a person being evil, this is a thoughtform. To annihilate this thoughtform you think about the same person being a good person. These two thoughtforms gradually annihilate each other and create a state in your mind which can be called a state of *indifference*.

The time needed for the destruction of these two opposing thoughtforms depends on the emotions you have toward the person.

It is possible to annihilate negative thoughtforms by deliberately creating thoughtforms in your mind that are opposites. This can be done by using your creative imagination. For example, if you feel that you yourself did something wrong and you built a negative thoughtform about yourself, you can annihilate that thoughtform by using your creative imagination and building an opposite thoughtform. You can do this by the following methods:

1. Create an imaginary life in which you are the most benevolent, wonderful person.

2. Do exactly the opposite of the wrong act that you did before.

3. "Burn" your negative thoughtform if that thoughtform is not an extension of an idea.

4. Practice scientific meditation. This method is the royal road to victory.[1]

---

1. For full information on meditation, see *The Science of Meditation, The Psyche and Psychism, and The Ageless Wisdom*, Ch. 26.

If a thoughtform is an extension of a lofty idea, that thoughtform may vanish for a while then build itself again, stronger than before. But most thoughtforms are the result of a formulation of events, our reactions and responses to people and conditions, or our interests, fears, and desires, and it is easy to annihilate them.

To "burn" a thoughtform you can use the laser light of your soul. The soul has seven rays, and each has its color, or together they are white. To use this "laser beam" you need training. The training takes some time.

The steps of training are as follows:

1. Sit in a comfortable position and imagine an object on a table. Project a beam of light through the center between your eyebrows. Make this light hit the object and annihilate it like a rocket.

2. Every day for three months choose an object and for five minutes try to burn the object and annihilate it. Very soon you will note that certain colors do the job better than others. Generally, the colors orange, ruby, and white are very destructive.

3. After three months, again imagine an object, and this time do the following:

   a. Project a beam of light and annihilate it. Then reform it.

   b. Destroy it and create a better form. At each sitting you must annihilate the object and recreate it at least ten times.

c. Try the same technique on your emotional objects or emotions. They also have forms that must be destroyed and rebuilt.

You can begin destroying forms or entire events of thoughtforms of fear, anger, hatred, jealousy, revenge, treason, etc. by working slowly on each one for at least one month.

Then take mental thoughtforms, such as

greed

sex

vanity

ego

various habits

separatism

fanaticism

fear

You can use your creative imagination to burn and annihilate each thoughtform's negative elements, or you can create their opposites.

Note that there are mental and emotional fears built by such elements.

Sometimes direct annihilation is easier if you are trained.

By using these two techniques, you can possibly strengthen yourself and wipe out negative and polluting elements from your nature. The more you clean your negative thoughtforms, the healthier you become.

Most of our negative thoughtforms pollute our nature over the years and create poison. Our nature gradually weakens, and sicknesses or diseases begin to develop.

The same happens to our emotional and mental worlds. As long as we nurture or nourish negative thoughtforms, our health suffers and our relations with other people and life in general become unhappy and destructive. Our mental activities lose their clarity and strength, and our responses become dull, slow, and inaccurate.

To be able to use such a procedure effectively you must practice for a long time. Gradually you will notice that you can make yourself

healthy

happy

prosperous

successful

You can gain control over your habits, urges, and drives. You can destroy your posthypnotic suggestions. You can control your emotions and thought patterns. This actually means that you save energy by preventing leakage and waste of energy and by generating energy.

Those who do not have clear thinking or quick mental responses are those whose mental mechanism is full of confusion or contradictory thoughtforms which cannot annihilate each other. Such a mental condition comes into being when one creates or collects thoughtforms that are contradictory to the thoughtforms built by and around great ideas, principles, and high standards.

Such thoughtforms both nourish your lesser or negative thoughtforms and disintegrate them, creating chaos in your nature.

By using the burning or balancing technique (creating opposite thoughtforms), you can eventually gain total control of your threefold mechanism. This is how you can be your Self. Every time you gain some control over your mechanism and its fluctuations, you become more your Self. Your Self is discovered and identified by gaining control of your mechanism, the not-self.

The beam of light that you can project through the center between your eyebrows can be used any hour of the day and even during sleep when in the Subtle Worlds. You can use it when you meet people, when you touch objects, when you eat food. But such a technique operates under a very potent law. The law says, **"If this beam of light is used to harm people or to protect evil intentions and control people, the beam reverses itself and burns the mechanism through which it is projected."**

To be able to activate the laser beam and gain control of this energy, you must obey the Law of Harmlessness and decide never to violate the karma and freedom of people.

The beam of light can be used to increase the awareness of people, to make your actions, words, and thoughts impressive, but not to violate their karma and freedom.

One must purify his own nature before he is allowed to help others to purify themselves.

This energy of light can be used also to annihilate dark forces around you in certain places and areas and to destroy entities that are sources of viruses and microbes.

You can destroy evil thoughtforms projected toward you in forms of hatred and slander. You can destroy accumulated negative energy around you produced by your past wrongdoings.

To do all this, you need training — self training. Regular, daily training eventually will bring you rewards that you did not anticipate and you become a tower of protection both for yourself and for others.

A thorough investigation shows how much turmoil we have within our mental world. Our mental world is like a radio tower broadcasting conflicting directions, conflicting announcements. Every day we fill our radio tower with negative and positive statements. One minute we identify with beauty, the next minute with ugliness. One minute we go right, next minute left. Thoughtforms produced by such actions accumulate in circuits that block our happiness, joy, clarity of mind, and the beauty of our vision. Such a condition creates the life we are living.

The condition in the world is exactly the reflection of the consciousness of the people in the world, complicated by the progressive energies radiating from advancing people and centers in the sphere of the world.

When the human consciousness attains freedom from the disturbances of the three lower worlds, it can contact higher forces and in a greater capacity serve humanity.

The first task is to purify your physical atmosphere. To do this, visualize material objects that can be stolen, destroyed, burned, or lost, for example:

valuables

money

documents

contracts

real estate

antiques

paintings

Through your imagination, create an event in which one of these items is stolen, lost, destroyed, or burned. Focus your eyes on that event and, projecting an orange beam of light, annihilate that event existing in your mind.

Do this exercise with at least ten objects daily, ten minutes for each object, destroying the event built around the object. Do this several times in ten minutes, burning and annihilating the event along with its associated fear.

The second phase is to discover fears related to the emotional nature generated by children, family members, friends; fears generated from sex; fears from relationships with friends, students, teachers; fears of not being loved, not being understood, not being accepted and appreciated. You can create ten dramas around the axis of such emotional fears and burn them with white light. Take ten minutes for each event.

Sometimes you do not need to fabricate events if you already have memories of factual experiences. Such experiences exist and create disturbances in you and in your relationships.

You can take one event per day or take three to ten events according to the time available. But never try to do this exercise if you do not have time, or if you are not serious.

Examples of emotional fears are events in which you failed, were humiliated, embarrassed, shamed; events in which you were emotionally upset, betrayed, cheated; a moment in which you lost your hope, your trust, your faith; a moment in which you were *lost*.

The third exercise will be for the destruction of fear in the mental body. There are many kinds of fears related to our mental body:

— fear of being ignorant

— fear of being ugly

— fear of being unsuccessful

— fear of death

— fear of failures and defeat

— fear of psychic attacks, obsession, possession

— fear of hell

— fear of rejection

With your creative imagination, try to create events around these elements and try to act in the drama. After you are really involved in the drama of the event, back away and destroy and annihilate the whole event with a silvery blue beam of light projected on the event from the middle point of your forehead.

During the creating of these events, various fears will emerge. Do not reject them. Make them part of the same event so that later you burn and annihilate them at the same moment with the whole event.

Remember that this is the first method and easier for those who are on the line of willpower.

The second is the balancing method by creating the opposing thoughtform which is charged with courage, joy, daring, and fearlessness. This is easy to do for those who are on the line of intellect or on the line of Third Ray action.

Each event created by you or existing in your memory must be played, and you must be involved in it as realistically as possible. Then destroy it by one of the methods explained above.

Never leave an event if it is not destroyed. Do the exercise again and again until all parts of that resisting event are totally annihilated. The reason for this is that any event not completely annihilated can quickly germinate, multiply, and grow, forming a huge obstacle on your path of future development and expansion. So, if it becomes necessary, try not to rest until the event under consideration is totally destroyed.

There are many thoughtforms that are

1. not completed

2. mixed

3. fabricated

4. reflected from other sources

5. encapsulated

These are thoughtforms which cloud the mental mechanism and often make its right function impossible.

The student of wisdom must try to use these methods to disperse such accumulations by

1. projecting light

2. balancing

3. increasing the positive, clear, factual thoughtforms to such a degree that the rest are assimilated or annihilated by them

Peace of mind — serenity of mind — is the cause of victory and happiness.

Through such exercises you may penetrate into your dungeon, your subconscious mind, and blow it out as if by dynamite. Such an event brings a major crisis in your life, but it also purifies the agelong accumulation in the stables of your subconscious realms.

Colors can be used in the visualizations as follows:

- An orange beam of light when you are destroying an outer object or event

- A white beam of light when you are trying to destroy thoughtforms, emotions, and dark or grey spots in your aura or in your etheric body

- Blue for healing, soothing, expanding

- Green for regeneration, action, strengthening

- Yellow for purification

- Violet for harmony, rhythm, relaxation

- Red for stimulation

- White for everything you need

After these exercises, use thirty minutes to create an event of *immortality* in which you are the master of time and space, the master of fire, flood, wind, volcanoes, and earthquakes.

Use thirty minutes to create an event of great *success*.

Use thirty minutes to create an event of great *beauty*.

Any time you are free from your daily obligations, visualize such events of immortality, success, and beauty. These will create a new center or source of energy within you from which will emanate currents of joy, enthusiasm, and courage.

In these three exercises, you can include all those whom you love.

Create a great event of *joy*. Let joy penetrate every part of your physical, emotional, and mental bodies. Let joy radiate to all your environment. Breathe, move, speak in joy.

One of the fears that strongly affects our life and sometimes even paralyzes our normal relationships with people is the fear of humiliation, or the fear we build during humiliation.

People, from three to eighteen years old especially go through many forms of humiliation. To express the state of their humiliation they use certain words such as having hurt feelings, embarrassment, feeling let-down, put-down, shamed, disgraced, feeling small, feeling cheap. Such feelings slowly develop corresponding thoughtforms and gradually handicap a person's spiritual growth and relationships.

Many young people are caught in such a network of humiliation. To liberate them from such a condition, at least once a year they must go through the procedure given in this chapter.

I have worked with many young ones, and, using these exercises, I saw one hundred percent improvement in their school work, in their relationships with their family members, and with their school environment and life in general.

Humiliation is a moment when you lose your self-respect, when you realize that you did something terribly wrong but you never admitted it. Humiliation is an experience of losing your existence, your prestige, your identity.

There is also another experience of humiliation in which people lie about you. Such a humiliation opens new fountains of energy within you to strive toward new heights. People may humiliate your reputation for their hatred and malice, but this does not make you lose your identity.

Humiliation also happens when you lie about someone. Then you realize how bad your lie was and how sorry you feel now.

One of my friends told me that he felt extremely humiliated whenever he became sick, whenever he went to the hospital for surgery or treatment. He said, "Every time I was sick I lost respect for myself." This was a very complicated feeling, and I wanted to know why he was feeling humiliated. One of my assumptions was that he felt that his sickness was the result of his breaking the moral or spiritual law or the result of his "sinning."

Another assumption was that as a soul he was ashamed of seeing the weakness and imperfection of his physical body.

The third assumption was that he felt humiliated in front of his friends for not being in good health and not keeping up with them.

Such humiliations are very real. For example, I had a great friend who lost his leg. From that moment on he never wanted anyone to see him. He felt deeply humiliated until in various ways he was helped to disidentify himself from his body and think about himself as a beautiful soul.

In the state of humiliation, one is wide open for many posthypnotic suggestions. The worst hypnotic suggestions are planted within our subconscious mind during the moments of humiliation. There are two sources of posthypnotic suggestions: outer and inner. In the state of humiliation, a person is open for attack from these two sources.

The humiliated person builds a seriously deteriorating self-image of himself, and every part of it sinks into the subconscious mind. Remember that a self-image is built from imagination, feelings, and thoughts — all of which go into the subconscious realms. This is why it is imperative that we do not humiliate people but, even in their lowest state of beingness, try to throw a spark of light which might in the future develop a bridge of salvation.

Real servants of light never condemn and forsake people for their failures, stupidities, nor even for their crimes but instead seek ways and means to lead them into light and self-respect.

Sometimes those who humiliate other people need more work than those who are humiliated because an urge to humiliate people is a sign that there is a very polluted and stagnated pool of consciousness within them. They need very extensive help to be released from this state of consciousness.

My Teacher used to bring such teenagers to his office and make them write down all the fears, humiliations, and embarrassments they had had in the past. Afterward he used to explain to them that their urge to humiliate other children was an urge especially to humiliate themselves.

People humiliate others to get even with their own humiliated self. This is a device to cover-up their stagnation. Sometimes my Teacher used to act like Jesus in reminding them of the "shaft in their own eye."

At the end of a session, you must do the following exercises for the final releasing procedure:

1. Visualize yellow light in the central point of your head. Make the yellow light — a yellow mist — spread all over your body, penetrating every part of it and evaporating through your fingers and toes.

2. Repeat this with a blue light.

3. Repeat this with a white light.

This allows the circulation of psychic energy and prana without any hindrance within your physical, astral, and mental vehicles and strengthens your aura to repel certain attacks coming from thoughtforms related to your former painful thoughtform.

If another person guided you for this whole procedure for so many hours, he will not be free from certain effects. As session after session continues, the words and the emotional and mental conditions of the subject will affect the guide, pulling out certain elements from his subconsciousness and bringing to the surface of his mind certain agitating elements. This is why every time the guide works on a subject, he must go through a self-conducted procedure to annihilate his own thoughtforms.

These are the steps for the guide to follow:

1. Sit relaxed and visualize a ruby point above your head.

2. Remember your session and burn out and annihilate through the beam of light radiating through that ruby point all thoughtforms built throughout the session.

3. This must be done at the end of each session.

4. Then repeat the exercises given to the subject for the total cleansing process.

5. Say the *Great Invocation* three times.

From the point of Light within the Mind of God
Let light stream forth into the minds of men.
Let Light descend on Earth.

From the point of Love within the Heart of God
Let love stream forth into the hearts of men.
May Christ return to Earth.

From the centre where the Will of God is known
Let purpose guide the little wills of men —
The purpose which the Masters know and serve.

From the centre which we call the race of men
Let the Plan of Love and Light work out
And may it seal the door where evil dwells.

Let Light and Love and Power restore the Plan on Earth.

Here are some suggestions to control fear:

1. Impose the fact upon your mind that you are an immortal being.

2. Face the object of fear and see how it acts as a tool of karma.

3. Face the fear and see if it can hurt your essence. In contrast, see how it can help your essence to actualize itself.

Remember your fearful experiences and try to relive them again and again in your imagination, seeing how powerless they are.

Remember that a fear is a patch of clouds in your eternal sky which is transient and cannot prevent your journey toward the Sun.

Fear is a thoughtform transmitting self defeating forces into you. Break the thoughtform, altering its painful formation into joyful scenes.

Destroy the form of the fear through the fiery energy of your soul.

Fear is an entity which can be discarded from your aura by increasing your joy and purity.

Fear can be

— mental

— emotional

— physical-material

Its nature must be as it is.

There are basic ideas on which one must stand:

1. You are Immortal.

2. Nothing can hurt you —

   not water

   not fire

   not earth

   not wind

   not enemies

   not time

3. No one can take away from you whatever *you have* in your essence. All properties that you have in the physical world exist in your essence. In astral and mental planes they are yours, and they will be yours when you come back to the physical plane.

4. All the love that you have will be yours in all coming lives. All the labor and service that you have started will increase in coming centuries.

5. Once you have, nothing can be lost.

   Once you know, no one can take that knowledge from you.

   Once you plan, it will actualize.

6. No one can stop your labor and service forever. It will run in a stronger flow.

But remember:

- All that you have must be the result of your *labor*.

- You will not steal or take away anything from others.

- All that you stole will go back to its true owners.

- All that you took by invasion will be taken away from you.

- All that will remain with you is that which you earned with your earnest, righteous labor — all that you earned by legal means.

- Things will be taken from you which you do not own in truth.

- If there is no true unity, you will be separated.

- All that will stay with you are those things which are truly yours and you paid for them.

- All that you are will remain with you.

- All that you are not will be taken from you.

- All that is your knowledge will stay with you.

- All that is not your knowledge will be taken from you.

If things are taken from you that do not belong to you legally, why be afraid? On the contrary, you must feel grateful when life takes away from you things that do not belong to you. That is the only way that you can have things that really belong to you.

Never be afraid that people will take things from you. All that is taken will come back to you with interest. Those who belittle you will be those who will labor hard to build your reputation and fame. Nothing real can be destroyed in you. People can destroy all that is fake in you, and this will help you in your real growth.

Slander and malice make people heavily indebted to you. In the future, their slander and malice toward you will be your savings in the bank — if you did not do the same to them.

To live in reality is to conquer fear. Eliminate fear from the corridors of your subconscious mind, from your thinking, from your memories. The less fear you have, the more victorious you will be.

A fearless life is a life lived by the will and plan of your soul.

Fear is attachment to those elements in you which do not belong to you. In detaching from things that do not belong to you, you discover that which is *you.*

Lord Krishna says in the Bhagavad Gita, "You are unbreakable, insoluble, and can neither be burned nor dried. You are everlasting, all-pervading, unchangeable, immovable, the same — eternally."

Time is an illusion. It has days, years, and vast cycles. But there is no time in

havingness

knowingness

beingness

service

life

These five do not have intervals. They are a continuous flow without interrupting the life current.

You do not start a service and then interrupt it by death or by other hindrances or attacks. It is not so. A service started continues forever here, there, everywhere you are. Service is your essence.

You do not start knowing, and then stop knowing. Your knowledge goes with you and continually increases.

You cannot achieve beingness and be interrupted. You continually have your beingness with you, like a thread that goes in and out of the fabric. Outside you see interruption, but inside it is one thread.

A man was killed while he was writing a poem. He will continue to write in the subtle worlds — and will continue when he comes back again in another incarnation.

Things that you start must reach their conclusion and purpose — unless you change their direction or essence.

Only your lies will be taken from you to help free you from your burden.

Your separatism will teach you how to be inclusive. Every separative act will lead you to those from whom you wanted to separate.

When you hate a nation because of its beauty and genius, you will be born in that nation with pain and suffering.

Most of your fears are from the fact that you see only one side of life. When you see both sides, fear disappears.

30 | The Subconscious and Past Lives

Many people these days are interested in their past lives, and some already "know" where and how they lived in the past.

The Ageless Wisdom never encourages people to discover or to be occupied with their past lives, but rather it encourages them to look to future possibilities and strive toward a glorious future.

The reason for this is that what we think of as our past lives are mostly

1. Fabrications of our desires, wishes, and dreams

2. Dramatizations of our thoughtforms

3. The mixture of events reflected in our astral mirror

4. Subconscious discharges

5. Identification with thoughtforms created by masses

It is seldom that a person contacts his past lives, and then it is under the supervision of a Master. Our past lives exist in the scrolls of Akasha, like a film, and we can have access to them after the Third Initiation when our subconscious mind is totally washed away and continuity of consciousness is achieved.

Our subconscious mind does not contain any sequence of events of our past lives. However, they exist in our three lower permanent atoms and in our Chalice. The "past lives" that we see are a combination of our wishful thinking, plus subconscious material collected in this lifetime mixed together with the many thoughtforms from others who think about us.

Through the law of association, all these come together and give us the impression that we are in contact with our past lives.

Sometimes we are hypnotically impressed by the events of a time and by its personnel. Such events and persons live in our subconscious and, even mixing with our individual image, become part of our individuality.

Some of the "past lives" originate from such impressions.

In some cases, when flashes of our past lives are discovered through association, we experience a real storm in our permanent atoms. This creates a very uncomfortable situation in our three bodies — if we are not yet an Initiate of Transfiguration.

Identification with thoughtforms created by the masses can have very tragic and humiliating consequences. We see people calling themselves Napoleon, Cleopatra, Jesus, St. Paul, St. John, etc.

These are very condensed thoughtforms in Space, and if someone is identified with one of them, he will have a very hard time getting free of it.

The identification with such powerful thoughtforms is based in our subconscious elements and especially in posthypnotic suggestions. Our subconscious is a part of the collective subconscious of the masses. Sometimes a subconscious event remains in its capsule and does not mix with the collective subconscious, but sometimes it does. During such a mixture, the mind goes berserk and the person demonstrates confusion, extreme fear, imbalanced behavior, and absent-mindedness. To protect himself from such a mental state, the person identifies himself with a hero figure and becomes the hero. The conflict between the consciousness and the subconscious mind stops, but the conscious mind, as if from a far distance, watches all that happens to the personality without having any power to interfere.

This hero image dramatizes all that exists in the subconscious mind until the person hurts his reputation, social relationships, and business and falls into a prison or asylum where they inject chemicals into him that make him insensitive to subconscious imagery.

Of course, it is possible to give psychological help to such a person when the drama is just beginning.

In a ten year period I spoke with five people claiming to be Jesus, one St. Paul, and one St. John. They really believed that they were the incarnation of these persons.

The most shocking experience for them is that, though they believe they are the hero they are identified with, they lack the power, the wisdom, and the talents these individualities expressed in the past. Of course, their subconscious mind has every kind of rationalization to convince them that it does not matter.

Often when they disidentify from their image or thoughtform, they feel very desperate, shamed, humiliated, lonely, and stupid. It is here that professionals are needed to rehabilitate them and bring their own consciousness into their brain.

Some of these people are mentally damaged for life. Some of them go insane, especially when an astral entity enters into the thoughtform they are identified with and possesses them for life. Such a person is almost incurable because the entity totally possesses the person and acts with a great amount of stupidity as if it were the historical individual.

Many people put themselves into such a danger by occupying themselves with past lives. It is true that past lives exist, but the revelation of psychics and mediums are, in most cases, lies. It is better not to believe them until you are in a state of enlightenment in which you can come in contact with your past lives, if it is absolutely necessary for you.

It is more probable that after the Third Initiation you will focus all your attention on the future.

Our preoccupation with the past calls out certain associated elements from our subconscious mind and stirs up our permanent atoms.

Some people fall into turmoil after their "past life" is revealed to them. They imitate queens, kings, soldiers, apostles, saviors, bankers, painters and impose on themselves an entirely false image. They become fake, unreal, and artificial.

Such behavior continues for a long time if they escape obsession or possession, but sooner or later the hard realities of life bring them to their senses.

There are those who know a few of their past lives — but such people have an extremely pure heart, lead a harmless life, and are full of compassion and joy.

There are people who, because of the purity of their astral body, see the reflections in it of the events registered in Akasha. It is very interesting to note that those who have this purity and have certain information about their past lives do not have the slightest interest in their past lives, and not a single element of their past lives has any influence on them.

Purity and enlightenment lead the consciousness toward the future.

When psychics tell us about our past lives, they really retard our progress toward the future, making us occupy ourselves with the past and forcing us to live according to the measures and habits of the "past life." Because what they say to us is an intelligent fabrication, we start building our future upon a nonexistent present, a nonexistent foundation.

31 | The Unconscious and the Superconscious

The unconscious domain is beyond the conscious. Our waking consciousness is normal to us, *if* we are really conscious. Generally we are not conscious on the astral or mental planes. They are unconscious fields for us. For those who are conscious in the mental plane, the Intuitional Plane is the Unconscious for them. Normally the Intuitional, Atmic, and higher planes are the unconscious domains.

The Unconscious is any higher plane to which we yet have no access, but it is the domain from which come new ideas, revelations, principles, visions, and energies to enrich our consciousness.

The Unconscious is a state of consciousness which does not exist for us because of our level of evolution.

The difference between the Unconscious and Superconsciousness is that we have access to the Superconsciousness through the Intuition and flashes of light. But the Unconscious does not exist for us due to the absence of the needed mechanism. The Superconsciousness is in our reach.

The Unconscious partially changes into the Superconscious when a portion of the Superconscious is conquered. As much as we are able to penetrate into the Superconscious, the availability of the Unconscious becomes possible.

The Unconscious surrounds us like an ocean. Our deep meditations create responses from the Unconscious. These responses reach us from the realm of the Superconsciousness.

Superconsciousness can be a part of consciousness if we build a steady focus of consciousness there, but most of the time the Superconsciousness is visited by intense efforts of meditation or even a brief moment of contemplation.

Through contemplation it is possible to enter into the superconscious realms and remember experiences lasting for a few seconds or hours. It is not possible to stay in a superconscious state unless one transcends his normal consciousness.

The resources for the great leaders and authorities in the seven fields of human endeavor are in the superconscious realms which they enter through meditation, contemplation, deep thinking, and sometimes in crises or in ecstasy, and bring back the light that guides their steps in their particular field of service.

The Unconsciousness remains beyond the consciousness and the Superconsciousness. Even if a person accidentally "falls" into it, he remembers nothing of it. The Unconscious has its own many levels, and on each level are found those who are conscious on that level. By establishing communication with such advanced beings, we gradually become conscious on these unconscious levels.

The subconscious is not a sphere of Unconsciousness, as some people suggest. The subconsciousness is always available to us. We have great power over it. We can play with it. But the Unconscious remains out of our reach, except if we penetrate into it after building the needed senses to be active in it. For a "fish," the unconscious planes are what exists beyond the sea or pool.

Many people are totally unconscious in the astral plane, and one cannot make them believe that there is an astral consciousness since for them it is an unconscious domain. But, when they eventually become active and awaken in the astral consciousness, they realize that it is a totally new territory for them.

The same thing is true for mental and intuitional unconsciousness. These are beyond the average person's consciousness.

For us, planetary consciousness is an unconsciousness. Solar consciousness and galactic consciousness remain beyond our consciousness. They are really unconscious domains for us, but it is these realms which enrich our life through their precipitations, impressions, principles, and inspirations.

For example, the Divine Plan and the Divine Purpose are in the domain of the Unconscious, but Their precipitations create in our consciousness new civilizations and new cultures.

The Unconscious is not the Superconscious. It is not racial consciousness or the collective consciousness.

Racial consciousness is the sum total of the consciousness that humanity, as a whole, has — which is predominantly physical level automatic consciousness. This is also the collective consciousness.

The fourth mental level consciousness has the faculty of conscious discrimination. For example, it chooses what to eat. But the assimilation mechanism then selects elements for certain parts of the body through an act of selection of which you are unconscious.

The assimilation mechanism which acts selectively and "consciously" — as it does things right — is the power of the positive side of the seventh level of the mind. Similarly, the selectivity and assimilation of the astral body is carried out by the positive side of the sixth level of the mental body. The positive side of the subconscious mind is the conscious mind itself with subconscious elements. The conscious mind becomes negative when it is filled with subconscious elements.

But humanity as a whole and nations as a whole both have their subconsciousness in which their past is buried, and both have their collective Chalice in which their hope for the future is found. They also have their Unconsciousness and their Superconsciousness, which are the next levels of consciousness that they are as yet unable to penetrate.

Those who have higher levels of consciousness act as bridges between conscious, unconscious, and superconscious domains and bring much light and guidance to humanity.

There are also those groups or individuals who are bridges between the collective subconscious and consciousness. They are those who bring elements from the subconscious that were hidden for ages, for example, dark rituals, animosity, fear, wars, revolutions, organized crimes, genocide, etc., and thus serve to clean the mess through destruction.

In a way such individuals act as embodiments of racial or global subconscious urges and drives and create painful upheavals on a global dimension.

Often the "higher bridge," through new ideas, visions, and principles, tries to offset or control the destructions brought about by the "lower bridges" by sealing the door of the collective subconsciousness of humanity and letting a new culture and civilization flourish all over the world.

All of the destructive and evil leaders are, in a sense, incarnations of the substances of the hatred, fear, jealousy, anger, and revenge of humanity plus of their own vanities and ego.

All such elements provide bodies for the dark ones who come to humanity to work out their karma, a karma which they created in their ignorance.

Humanity pays a heavy taxation in serving separatism, totalitarianism, fear, hatred, revenge, jealousy, vanity, and ego.

Cyclically, the subconsciousness of humanity throws out all such elements, providing bodies for the dictators — Hitlers, Neros, and Stalins — and the other leaders of separatism and materialism appearing almost in every country.

As the subconsciousness of a human being creates the drama of an individual life, so also the collective subconsciousness of humanity creates a global tragedy when it erupts like a volcano.

On the other hand, the collective Chalice of humanity provides those elements which serve as the body of the great Messengers and Heroes who appear in the world to lead humanity toward higher levels of understanding and existence. Humanity worships such Heroes and Saviors who appear in the world vested with the treasury of the collective Chalice of humanity. Those helping humanity are protected by the treasury of their own Chalice, and they rise above the abyss of the collective subconscious.

32 | The Subconscious and Barriers

The subconscious mind has the tendency to hold people at their present level and not let them make breakthroughs. It is in the subconsciousness that the barriers to future progress and unfoldment of the person exist. Unless we overcome these barriers prevalent in present ideologies, religions, and educational systems, we will resist any changes, even when we feel that they are outdated.

All religions and educational institutions are built or formed to answer the needs and the level of certain people. If these religions and educational institutions claim that they are the only way to meet all the needs for all levels, then they are totalitarian institutions. As such, they operate under the assumption that the need or the level of people never changes nor rises. This is how ideologies and religions and educational institutions become at certain times obsolete and outdated after becoming for a long time a barrier to the evolution of people connected with them.

In the progressive development of human consciousness, barriers must be removed and a new level of expansion of consciousness, new needs, and new levels must be met.

Thus, ideologies, religions, and educational organizations must be like paths through which people pass toward new stations of consciousness instead of becoming dead-end streets.

The contents of the subconscious mind are retrogressive, in general, and these contents feed or nourish those thoughts and thoughtforms that are retrogressive. In turn, those nourished and fed thoughts and thoughtforms weaken and kill all those thoughts which have the fire of progressive tendencies. Thus, the negative thoughtforms increase in the conscious mind if the positive thoughts are not strengthened and multiplied through meditation and through personal contact with the Teacher.

A Teacher not only supports and feeds the creative and positive thoughts in our mind but also protects, by his or her aura, those thoughtforms and makes them dynamic and aggressive against the negative currents of the subconscious mind.

When a person's mental plane turns negative, it chooses or creates those ideologies, those religions, or those educational concepts that are retrogressive, limiting, separative, and destructive. Such a mental state eventually opens all channels of the subconscious mind and breaks down all resistances. Such conditions are often seen in individuals who supported their own negative or retrogressive attitudes of mind. Often, they were led into asylums after certain destructive and criminal behaviors.

Efforts to actualize our constructive and creative thoughts either destroy the negative thoughts or change their nature. This is why Teachers advise us not only to try to have certain knowledge about ideologies, educational methods, and religions but also to actualize those parts of the ideologies, educational methods, and religions which are positive, constructive, creative, and inclusive. Certain people cannot discriminate between these two paths.

There are two ways of walking on the path. One is the intellectual path with endless speculations of reality and unreality, objects and subjects, fullness and emptiness; and the other is the path of beingness, unfoldment, and expansion.

The first path is lost in the jungles of mental hallucination; the other path continually advances, going from within to without. This is the path of no arguments and debates. It is the path of actualization.

Many people have created mountains of literature about emptiness, voidness, fullness, self, not self, etc., etc. but have never actualized anything. They think playing with words makes them progress.

The path of actualization is mastery and the expansion of consciousness. Mastery is freedom from all physical, emotional, and mental limitations. Expansion of consciousness means the ability to relate in our higher bodies and in higher dimensions.

People can sit for one thousand years and argue about the nature of patience or creativity but never experience patience, nor prove their creativity. Such people delay travelers from achievement.

Arguments on philosophical topics have some Eastern people far behind in their evolution and usefulness. Arguments on religious subjects have kept people in the West from actualization of the spirit of religion.

We have the wrong idea that the East is religious. It is not; it is philosophical. The West is religious. If you study Tibetan, Chinese, and Indian literature, you will see how many millions of tons of mental stuff they used for their philosophical arguments. The same is true for the West in regard to religion.

Between these two systems there are the universal revelations which are the myths of all nations, East and West, and the sciences of all nations, East and West. Myths balance philosophy and science balances religion.

The progress of man is not conditioned by the fabrications of his mind but by the expansion of his consciousness and by his increasing inclusiveness.

The progress of a man is proved by his four actions:

1. He lives to remove the pains and sufferings of other people.

2. He educates people to do the same.

3. He lives to make people discover the ultimate source of creativity in them and in Nature.

4. He helps other people to do the same.

These are his four paths, which are inclusive and without limit.

Though such a person tries to remove pain and suffering from the world and eliminate their causes, he also cultivates the joy of unfoldment and progress toward a beingness where joy and unfoldment permeate all his activities.

Such a person understands the value of all forms in Nature and enjoys the pleasures gained from them. And he makes people discover the source of light, love, and willpower in themselves and in Nature. The discovery of this source makes a person radioactive, fragrant, magnetic, and a beam of light shining upon the path of humanity. Only such a man can empty his subconscious elements and use them as fuel for his creative achievements.

33 | Nations and the Subconscious Mind

As we have times when our subconsciousness is restimulated and surfaces, so too have the nations, humanity, the globe, and the solar system. At special times the national subconscious mind erupts and by a chain reaction makes the subconscious mind of humanity erupt. Such an event is called an "Armageddon" in which everybody loses his head and the masses act like patients in an asylum. They kill and they butcher each other. All their vices come to the surface and, under a banner of human rights, they destroy each other, all the while promising a future era of safety and peace.

It is important to know that as the subconscious mind of a man may lead him into destruction, the same is true of a nation and of humanity as a whole.

One day we will read the history of Space and know that many globes and solar systems annihilated themselves through the eruptions of their subconscious mind because the leaders sowed the seeds of murder, fear, hatred, jealousy, revenge, and destruction and loaded the subconscious mind of each individual of the planet and system.

The Universe has its cycles, and in a given cycle the individuals, nations, and humanity must clean their stables in a Herculean manner. If they do not, Nature will cleanse them and their stables to help the globe and solar system go through their own evolution, if they are not already contaminated to a critical degree.

We must also be aware that sometimes humanity is a victim of subconscious influences coming from Space. Such influences are very powerful and affect civilizations and cultures. Those who are heavily loaded with their own subconscious contents are swept under the destructive currents.

Those who have unfolded Chalices stay on top of the destructive waves and surf upon them, sometimes even becoming the saviors of our globe.

If you read history carefully, you will see that the destruction of Races, such as Lemuria and Atlantis, and the destruction of nations were the result of their accumulated subconscious mind. The more you fill your subconscious mind, the less sanity you have and the poorer your chances for survival.

Read the history of lost nations and you will find that before their destruction they were living in a state of physical, moral, and spiritual degeneration.

We think we are so civilized. But we have not left any place on the earth that is unpolluted. We have more sophisticated instruments to kill each other. The epidemic of crime and insanity is everywhere.

Are these the signs of a civilization or of barbarians?

The reason is the same: We have filled our subconscious mind, through our televisions, books, newspapers, magazines, fear, and pressure, with anti-survival materials. We do not even become surprised if our twelve year old boy makes a fourteen year old neighbor pregnant.

Bit by bit, all abnormal, unnatural things now seem to us to be natural and proper, even if we talk against them.

The greatest danger in the world is the increasing power of the subconscious mind, with its hidden weapons of hypnotic suggestions.

It is the subconscious mind that produces not only disturbances, karma, and conflict in our lives but also natural disasters, wars, and economic calamities.[1]

---

1. See also *Earthquakes and Disasters, What the Ageless Wisdom Tells Us.*

34 | An Advanced Exercise

In certain schools in the Far East, methods were given to dissolve the subconscious mind. One of these methods is to do the following exercise:

1. Relax and shut off every kind of thinking.

2. Wait in silence until the subconscious elements come to the surface and begin their parade.

3. Watch them with absolute detachment and indifference until they fade away.

If you are scared or excited by watching the subconscious parade, stop for a while and remember that they are not real but only a phantasmagoria. Do not be attached to them. Let them perform their drama — ugly, humorous, painful, scary — never mind. Watch them as you watch the clouds in the sky. Do not accept them as real. Do not make them real. Just observe. This may take one hour or two hours. Do this every day without hurry or the slightest excitement.

This not only burns away many of the elements of the subconscious mind but also cures the threefold lower bodies of the personality of many ailments. As long as these elements remain in the bodies, they exercise tremendous pressures on them.

As relaxation goes deeper and one learns to stand detached and observe the parade of the subconscious mind, the psychic energy increases and revitalizes the whole system and charges it with a fiery immunity.

But this is not too easy to learn. It takes sometimes weeks, sometimes years to learn this exercise. Once it is learned, one can daily clean a portion of his subconscious mind and related problems from the bodies.

One day it will be proven that the roots of most of our diseases are hidden in the subconscious mind. Also, it will be discovered that as the subconscious mind loses its elements, the energies of the Chalice penetrate deeper into the bodies or vehicles to heal them of every kind of trouble.

The way of longevity will be found in the Chalice; even the secret of immortality will be revealed in the Chalice.

As relaxation continues and tension circuits are annihilated, the psychic energy will circulate in the system with pranic fire and revitalize energies, heal and renew all tissues and organs, and cast out all that weakens the human vehicles.

With the above exercise, one must begin an exercise of deep breathing.[1] This must be done when the first exercise is mastered. After it is mastered, the person, during his relaxation, must begin to breathe very deeply during the exercise. This will not be easy for a while, but gradually the breathing will be very natural during relaxation.

After these two steps are taken, one must start adding the next exercise. The steps are as follows:

1. Do the three steps of the first exercise.

2. Add deep breathing.

3. Add this visualization:

   a. Visualize a blue electric fire in the heart center, six inches away from the middle point between the shoulder blades.

   b. After the blue fire is seen, visualize the blue fire penetrating into all the cells of the body and building a sphere of blue light around the body.

   c. Sit in that sphere, unmoved, silent, totally relaxed, and in great joy.

This is a supreme exercise which will reward those who do it with real faith and joy. The reward will be beyond their imagination.

---

1. See Chs. 53 and 54 of *New Dimensions in Healing* for further information on deep breathing.

Before you do this exercise, ask permission from your doctor and go slowly, gradually, and step by step. Do not hurry. Do not be discouraged if you cannot keep mentally silent, or if you cannot be detached from the subconscious parade. Keep on in your exercise, and you will see that you are learning the art. It is an art and it is a science.

The trick is not to think but to observe, to observe in total detachment and indifference as if you were watching a landscape from your window. It is difficult not to become involved with subconscious elements, but it is possible. You must make your exercise possible if you want to enter the path of liberation.

PART II

The
Chalice

The subject of the Chalice is not familiar to general readers. Efforts have been made to present it portion by portion to help people build an entire picture of the Chalice in their consciousness by their own efforts and striving.

If questions visit your mind, be patient. Maybe in the next chapter they will be answered. For more advanced teaching about the Chalice, please refer to *A Treatise on Cosmic Fire* by Alice A. Bailey.

Words of Wisdom
from a Great Sage

All threads which issue from the Chalice lead to action which is linked with the Spatial Fire.[1]

When the Chalice is filled with fire, the aura attracts the force of the Magnet.[2]

The knowledge of the Chalice very often brings anguish. Indeed, the planet is bathed in human tears.[3]

Only when the spirit can build the step of cumulation of the Chalice can he become a co-worker of the Cosmic Magnet.[4]

Of course, the treasury of the spirit is the Chalice. . . .[5]

---

1. Agni Yoga Society, *Infinity*, Vol. II (New York: Agni Yoga Society, 1957), para. 201.
2. *Ibid.*, para. 217.
3. *Ibid.*, para. 318.
4. *Ibid.*, para. 325.
5. *Ibid.*, para. 34.

When the consciousness awakens, the Chalice resounds.[6]

The Chalice is the repository of everything loved and precious.[7]

As a synthesized center, the Chalice preserves the most essential, indescribable accumulations.[8]

Therefore, he who carries the Silvery Lotus in his Chalice awakens through his vibrations the accumulations in others. The creativeness of the white ray is replaced by the radiance of the Silvery Lotus.[9]

The center of the Chalice gathers all creative threads. Therefore, each cosmic vibration resounds within the Chalice.[10]

From the Chalice issue all creative laws and in the Chalice are gathered all cosmic manifestations. Therefore, the enrichment of the Chalice affords realization of all cosmic plans. The foundations are gathered in the Chalice....[11]

6. *Ibid.*, para. 69.
7. Agni Yoga Society, *Brotherhood*, para. 464.
8. *Ibid.*, para. 463.
9. *Infinity*, Vol. 2, para. 131.
10. *Ibid.*, para. 152.
11. *Ibid.*, para. 192.

35 | The Chalice

The Teaching about the Chalice comes from the Atlantean Adepts. Before the submergence of Atlantis, the Adepts took this Teaching to India and then to the Himalayas.

The Teachers of humanity at first gave very little information about the Chalice. Using various symbols, They hinted about the Chalice in instructions to Their disciples. It was in 1922 that a Sage from the Himalayas gave an extensive and magnificent Teaching about it through dictations to Alice A. Bailey.

The Teaching says that in every human being there is a mechanism in the higher mental plane which registers all that happens to him and around him that is related to Beauty, Goodness, Righteousness, Joy, Freedom, Striving, and Sacrificial Service. In addition, all real wisdom and knowledge are accumulated in the Chalice. Great memories from past lives are also accumulated there. Another Sage says that the Chalice also contains some information communicated from Space.[1]

Such accumulations form the true treasury in the human being which can be used when a person consciously comes in contact with that treasury or when the Hierarchy gives an impulse and connects the treasury with the brain of the person. This wisdom is used in writing important books, dramas, stories, poems, in painting pictures, in composing music, and in making new discoveries and inventions.

This treasury accumulates age after age, life after life, and through coordination, association, and synthesis, it forms the fountainhead of wisdom and knowledge which manifests through the labor of geniuses in the world.

The Chalice is like the hard disk of our computer but with a very subtle and complicated mechanism.

The richer the Chalice is, the more influence it has in the life of the person. The poorer the content of the Chalice, the less influence it has in the life of the person.

As one progresses on the spiritual Path, he begins to have more access to the treasury. This slowly changes his life, and a day comes when the person inherits all the treasure found in his Chalice. He becomes an example of Beauty, Goodness, Righteousness, Joy, Freedom, Striving, Sacrificial Service, and Wisdom.

The consciousness of disciples and initiates is continuously fed by this treasury. If you are one of them, or if you are familiar with the biographies of great disciples

---

1. For an introductory chapter on the Chalice, please refer to *The Science of Becoming Oneself*, "The Chalice and the Seeds."

and initiates, you will see how the treasury of the Chalice manifests in life as

> — A source of direct knowledge
>
> — A sudden hint advising direction
>
> — Inspiration
>
> — Impression
>
> — Guidance
>
> — Discovery
>
> — Creativity
>
> — Intuitive ideas
>
> — Wisdom

Sometimes we say, "He is a rich man; he has a rich and wealthy consciousness," because the consciousness of such a man is like a meadow blessed by the occasional precipitation of the Chalice.

The content of the Chalice is very powerful because it affects many sides of our life and resonates with the Chalices that are blooming in each human being, in each Planetary, Solar, and Galactic Life. The Chalice is the current in the Universe which radiates benevolent influences in all spheres according to the wealth of the treasury.

Not only does every human being have a Chalice, but also each Planetary, Solar, and Galactic Life has a Chalice of Its own. The substance of our Chalice is given by our Solar Angel, but it is we who build up the Chalice with the most advanced atoms from our higher nature.

The petals of the Chalice of the Planetary Logos are formed of very advanced entities, according to their petals and to their evolution. The petals of the Chalice of the Solar Logos are built of entities equal to the ranks of the Planetary Logoi. The petals of the Chalice of the Galactic Logos are built of lives equal to the Solar Logoi. On each level, the building units of the petals of the Chalices are progressively

— More advanced

— Have more complicated responsibilities

— Have a broader or wider sphere of influence

— Deal with more powerful energies

— Have a vision which extends deeper into the Purpose of the Most High

The higher the Chalice is, the wider the sphere of its communication.

We must mention that on the human level not all the Chalices are active. Some of them have only a few petals that are open halfway. Others have more petals open according to the level of their evolution. Similarly, higher Chalices are in the process of being built.

Human Chalices are destroyed and their treasures are transferred to the Spiritual Triad at the Fourth Initiation. The Chalice of the Planetary Logos will be destroyed during Its Fourth Cosmic Initiation. The same is true for the Chalice of the Galactic Logos.

In comparison to the Chalice of the Galactic Logos, our Chalice lasts a few seconds. The Chalices of Great Lives in Space last for immeasurable eons.

All Great Chalices, as well as human Chalices, radiate their treasures into Space on the plane where they are found. As the human consciousness advances, it tunes to such treasures and uses them in creative labor. There are many ways of contact:

— Resonance

— Impression

— Inspiration

— Fusion

— Telepathy

— Direct or conscious contact

The contact through resonance is very natural and very often unconscious. Resonance manifests as sudden joy, an urge to do something great, a sudden vision, a sudden breakthrough. Chalices on all levels have an opportunity to resonate with higher Chalices and receive benevolent currents of energy according to their unfoldment.

Every contact, again according to the stage of the development of the Chalice, can affect us physically as physical happiness and health; emotionally as joy, uplifting feelings, peace, and love; mentally as creative thinking, understanding, power of analysis, creativity, intuitional visions, revelations, inclusiveness, synthesis, and the power of healing, enlightening, and encouraging.

On physical, emotional, and even on mental levels, all this resonance is often unconscious until at least six petals are unfolded in our Chalice.

There are many benefits of knowing about the Lotus or the Chalice.

1. Thinking and talking about the Chalice is equal to building or stimulating, developing or unfolding the Chalice within our consciousness and mind.

2. Knowing about it means to know what we are, what we need, and what is available to us.

3. In knowing about the Chalice, we discover how to use it to make our evolution progress in the best way possible.

4. In knowing about it, we discover how to use it intelligently to understand the mysteries of life and consciousness.

5. In knowing about it, we discover the future awaiting us on planetary and solar levels, and we learn how to fill our future Chalices with spiritual treasures.

Higher psychic powers are developed by the radioactivity and treasures of the Chalice. That is why true esotericism does not encourage us to follow artificial yogas and exercises to develop our psychic powers.

The true Teaching says that our higher psychic powers must be the result of our meditation, service, and sacrifice for the Common Good. Once the Chalice is filled, the fullness manifests as higher psychic powers in our future lives. The more we think about the Chalice, the more we stimulate it and magnetically draw more energy from the Solar Angel. This energy helps us live in a way that we accumulate more treasures for our Chalice. But if our lower bodies are not refined and integrated and aligned, the stimulation creates difficulties in our moods and relationships. This is why this science was kept a secret until 1922. The Great Teachers decided that this information would not be too dangerous due to the rapid development of the human being since that period.

As a safeguard for this precious information, the Teaching was scattered and written in such a way that window-shoppers would not be interested. We have not seen anyone writing about this science or discussing it in intellectual circles, groups, or churches. Very few have been interested in it.

36 | Names of the Chalice

Throughout centuries the Chalice was called by many different names but without giving any substantial details. For example, it was called

1. Chalice

2. Lotus

3. Bag

4. Purse

5. Treasury

6. Temple

7. Temple of Solomon

8. Temple Not Made by Hands

9. Causal Body

10. Sanctuary

11. Wheel of Fortune

12. Seat of Grace

13. Medicine Bag

14. Holy Grail

15. The Kingdom of God

In various teachings, religions, and traditions you can find these names.

For a clairvoyant the Chalice is a reality. For a psychologist it is the best device that explains highly complicated and obscure things in the psyche of man. For a scientist it is a great field of research.

Let us discuss these names in more detail.

1. **Chalice:** Contains the blood, the life essence, the Spirit.

2. **Lotus:** A growing and unfolding center with twelve petals in specific colors. The petals are like fiery flames.

3. **Bag:** Collects precious elements and keeps them in safety.

4. **Purse:** Bag that is with man as his life support.

5. **Treasury:** Container of all past victories, achievements, and heroic works; full of ideas, wisdom, and beauty collected throughout ages.

6. **Temple:** Where the Most High, the Jewel dwells.

7. **Temple of Solomon:** Built on the archetypes of higher planes.

8. **Temple Not Made by Hands:** That which is built by Solar Pitris and lunar pitris through the striving of man.

9. **Causal Body:** That which carries with it the physical, emotional, and Mental Permanent Atoms — the recordings of which determine the nature and bodies of our future incarnations.

10. **Sanctuary:** Where people enter for transformation, elevation, and contact with the Most High.

11. **Wheel of Fortune:** Where the contents of the Chalice, once contacted, provide us with every kind of prosperity.

12. **Seat of Grace:** Our savings account which helps us in our dire need.

13. **Medicine Bag:** Where all elements that protect us, give us good fortune, heal us, and make us find favors are found.

14. **Holy Grail:** Which collects knights for service and inspires them to dedicate themselves for the redemption of humanity.

15. **The Kingdom of God:** Where order, harmony, beauty, peace, cooperation, and glory are found.

37 | What is the Chalice?

The Chalice is found on the higher mental plane.

The mental plane is like a sphere around our head, the base of which reaches our throat center.

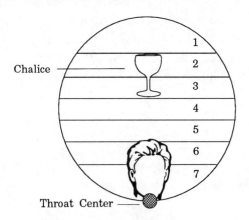

Diagram 37-1 The Mental Plane   235

The mental body is a mixture of five fires:

- The fire of the Seventh Ray

- The fire of the Sixth Ray

- The fire of the Fifth Ray

- The fire of the Fourth Ray

- All merged with the greater fire of the Third Ray

These produce the mental fire or the manas. It is in this substance that the planting and growth of the Chalice takes place. It is the Third Ray that makes the mental body spheroidal, revolving on its axis, which is in reality the Jewel in the Lotus. The Great Lords of these five Rays (7,6,5,4,3) gave Their own chemistry to build a device, the manas, which as millenniums passed became a highly organized device around the Chalice.[1]

Highly developed minds are able to bring down the treasures of the Chalice to the brain and make them tangible to humanity under the forms of creativity in all fields. The mental fire penetrates into all manifested forms, from the atom to the galaxies. Every atom, every cell, every form is endowed with the mental substance. This is the *nous* of the Greeks, the all pervading mind substance — the manas.

---

1. For information on the Seven Rays, please see the video *The Seven Rays Interpreted* with Torkom Saraydarian.

38 | Formation of the Chalice

The formation of the Lotus or the Chalice is the result of the labor of the Solar Angel Who builds the Lotus out of Its substance. We are told that when the Solar Angel descends into the mental plane, nine whirlpools come into being. These nine whirlpools are called "vibratory impulses."

The Solar Angels bring five impulses which together with four impulses from the seventh, sixth, fifth, and fourth subplanes of the mental plane form the number nine. These nine petals, though radiating a certain amount of light, remain like a closed bud for a long time.

On the mental plane, due to the presence of the Solar Angel, we see the formation of that fiery triangle which is called the Manasic Triangle.

This triangle is formed by the mental unit, the central point of the Lotus, and by the Mental Permanent Atom. As the fire circulates within this Manasic Triangle due to our meditation and sacrificial service, it slowly invokes the light of the Intuitional Plane. Eventually a stream of light reaches the center of the Lotus and creates three more petals around the Jewel in the Lotus. These three petals remain closed until the Fourth Initiation.

The Manasic Triangle increases in light and power and eventually turns into the Path — the Antahkarana — uniting the mental unit, the Chalice, and the Mental Permanent Atom.

This is yet the first part of the Antahkarana, which must penetrate even higher and connect the human soul to higher permanent atoms until the Monad is reached.

The Lotus is built around the human soul which was individualized at the Lemurian time when the Solar Angels came.

Before the Solar Angels came, man was not individualized, which means he had no "I" consciousness. He was a Monad — which was like a ray passing through all planes and reaching the physical body, centering itself in the heart.

Solar Angels are responsible for creating an identity on the ray of the Monad and making man *be*. The human soul is a knot on the ray of the Monad equipped with "I am" consciousness.

It took many thousands of years for the Solar Angels to create this "I am" consciousness. The process of formation of the "I am" consciousness, or the human soul, is called individualization.

After individualization, the human soul — who in his essence is the Monad — learns how to control his physical, emotional, and mental bodies which are built around the archetype created by the Solar Logos in the Cosmic Mental Plane, projected to the etheric plane, and by the labor of devas are then brought into existence as a human form.

The Solar Angel's duty is to make the human soul sensitive to Its wisdom and try to organize, coordinate, and master the organism given to him; to make the human soul clearly conscious of his own identity and unfold the glory hidden in his Core which is the Divine Monad, his Essence.

But until the human souls become fully individualized and self-conscious, it is the Solar Angels Who "run the show." They act as the man himself and, in the meantime, try to form the human soul. However, They are conditioned by the elements of the three vehicles of the human being and by their responses and reactions to life.

Through the first, second, and Third Initiations, the human soul achieves self-identity and successfully controls his physical, emotional, and mental bodies. Now the man is a human soul who has the divine treasury within himself, if he strives enough and brings it into manifestation.

His duty does not end there. He must not only organize and develop his physical, etheric, astral, and mental vehicles, but also he must build the higher vehicles, which are constructed of the substances of the Intuitional, Atmic, Monadic, and Divine Planes. And when his higher bodies are built, the human soul, as an individuality, can conquer time and space in the world, in the solar system, and eventually in the galaxy.

It is after individualization that the monadic ray gains self-consciousness, and he enters into the wheel of reincarnations.

The first and second Races and the first half of the Lemurian Race did not die or incarnate because there was no entity in the human form. There was only the Monad, which was not an entity but a ray.

After individualization the long pilgrimage of the human soul began. He incarnated again and again under the supervision of the Solar Angel and collected experience in each incarnation. He began to gain knowledge, wisdom, and experience as the human soul. This is why each human soul's age is different. There are old souls, there are young ones, and there are babies.

Old souls are those who, because of their good karma, incarnated and lived long years in each life and collected precious knowledge, experience, and wisdom.

Young ones are those who, because of their bad karma, lived short lives on earth and remained a very long time in Subtle Worlds in half-sleep states. Old souls do not waste time in the Subtle World but come to earth and continue their duties and responsibilities.

At the Fourth Initiation, we are told, our Solar Angel leaves us and we travel the Path alone.

In the Ageless Wisdom we are also told that there is even a possibility that this human soul, the real man, can fall into the tragedy of dissolution if for a long time he refuses to live in the principles of Beauty, Goodness, Righteousness, Joy, and Freedom. This is called the annihilation of the human soul.

It is the greatest disaster for a human soul when he dissolves in the chaotic forces of the Universe. His soul, like a patch of clouds, disappears in the ocean of Space, and his past video tapes play for a long time in the dimensions of Space and then melt away as if they had no previous existence.

39 | Man as Monad

Man is a Monad, a drop of fire of the Creative Force in the Universe. This fire, the Monad, throughout many ages and many creations, learns how to build a body of its own and gradually becomes a unit of the plant kingdom. After many millions of years, it graduates to the animal kingdom and then to the human kingdom, building along the way a better mechanism to contact the environment of each kingdom. At the beginning of the human kingdom, this Spark or Monad was found in a center called the *base of spine.*

There are very skilled builders in Space who are called Solar Pitris and lunar pitris. These are certain angels or devas who help human beings build their physical and subtle bodies and the Chalice. Actually, the substance of the Chalice is provided by Solar Angels in order to build the petals as the spiritual striving of the human being increases.

In the infancy of the human race on this planet, the human beings were like animals and they did not have a Chalice. But during the middle of the Lemurian Race, 18,000,000 years ago, Solar Angels came to earth in three different waves. The first group departed, but Their contact with humans indirectly energized the mental substance in man. The second wave of Angels came and put a substance in man which later developed into the Lotus. The third wave of Solar Angels came and entered into the substance left by the previous Solar Angels and used it as Their anchorage in the higher mental plane of man.

The developing Chalice was like a seed which, as it grew, turned into a Lotus flower. As the Lotus flower began to unfold, the Spark from the base of spine traveled upward on the etheric spine and eventually located itself in the center of the Lotus like a baby in the bosom of the Solar Angel.

The infusion between the Solar Angel and the human soul or Monad reaches its summit at the time of the Third Initiation. At this time we call the human Spark or the Monad the real human soul.

Of course we must remember that the process of the arrival of Solar Angels, the development of the Chalice, and the journey of the Monad has taken millions of years.[1] Thus the unfoldment of the Chalice takes centuries of effort, striving, discipline, meditation, and service.

---

1. For further information please refer to *The Science of Becoming Oneself*, pp. 63-75; *The Science of Meditation*, pp. 47-55; *Cosmos in Man*, pp. 177-200; *Other Worlds*, pp. 519-550; and *The Solar Angel*.

As the petals unfold, our physical, emotional, and mental bodies develop and organize and coordinate with each other so that the progress of the Spark continues until it reaches the center of the Lotus.

Each tier of the petals penetrates into one of our three bodies.

Our Chalice has twelve potential petals:

1. Three outermost petals called knowledge petals, which are composed of one knowledge petal, one love petal, and one sacrifice petal

2. Three love petals, which are composed of one love petal, one knowledge petal, one sacrifice petal

3. Three closer to the center called sacrifice petals, which are also composed of one sacrifice petal, one knowledge petal, one love petal

4. The fourth tier of petals — or the bud — does not show significant unfoldment until the Third Initiation is over and the human soul enters into the Fourth Initiation. This bud hides the Jewel

In this way knowledge, love, and sacrifice petals penetrate into each body of the personality.

Since we have knowledge, love, and sacrifice petals which penetrate into each body, we then have

A. On the physical plane

One knowledge-knowledge petal

One knowledge-love petal

One knowledge-sacrifice petal

B. On the astral plane

One love-knowledge petal

One love-love petal

One love-sacrifice petal

C. On the mental plane

One sacrifice-knowledge petal

One sacrifice-love petal

One sacrifice-sacrifice petal[2]

Each petal is an electric tube which has many functions as it unfolds.

As the petals unfold they bring forth the energy and wisdom of the Solar Angel.

Second, they bring into your bodies the treasures of the Chalice — past experiences, wisdom, beauty, etc.

Third, they bring the electric power of your inner essence. Also, each petal is destined to put the Jewel in the Lotus in contact with one of the constellations of the Zodiac.

The petals also key themselves in with the greater petals of greater Chalices and bring high-level electrical or fiery nourishment to the person. They are like trans-

---

2. The three petals of A are called knowledge petals, of B are called love petals, of C are called sacrifice petals.

mitters or speakers which transmit to the air all of your thoughts, feelings, and actions that are related to true sacrifice, love, and pure knowledge. Thus as the Chalice unfolds, Space is filled with the "fragrance" of the Chalice. Such a fragrance is used as food for many kinds of devas and as a source of inspiration for other living human beings.

Thus, the Chalice pulls the consciousness of man up to itself.

When the man and his consciousness are in the Chalice, the petals protect him and nourish him as if he were an embryo in the womb of the Lotus.

Each Chalice emanates color, light, and sound. As your Chalice unfolds, devas and Masters begin to notice it.

M.M. speaks about His garden and flowers. His garden is in the higher mental and Intuitional Planes where He notices the appearance of lotuses, lilies, or roses — the Chalices — as they grow and unfold.

Once a Chalice unfolds and thereby catches the attention of Great Ones, They watch it with special care. Sometimes They drop a few jewels in it. Sometimes They let a few jewels go to the brain of the person to be used in a time of need. Sometimes They measure the petals and their colors to see in what way and degree they are unfolding.

Each unfolding Lotus becomes a flower in Their garden that is well tended.

To be a flower in Their garden is a great achievement. It is a great opportunity to have contact with Great Ones and with fellow flowers.

One of the greatest ways to make the petals of the Chalice unfold is to develop the feeling of Brotherhood, a deep spiritual feeling that all living forms — visible or invisible — are our brothers. We are told that once a person develops the requirements of Brotherhood and establishes brotherly ties with others, he develops a line of contact between his physical brain and astral and mental realities. Such a line of contact unites him with the threefold planes of his brothers. But this is in the worldly sense.

Brothers never separate in the physical world, nor if they enter the astral world or the mental world. The line of contact created in them transcends the worlds, and they are always impressed by each other's condition and striving.

This is why Brotherhood is not only a source of joy, protection, support, and success, but also it is an imperative step leading to the Higher Worlds, discipline, trust, cooperation, and labor.

The formation of real Brotherhood brings each human soul closer to his own Chalice and makes him a cell in the group Chalice.

40 | Greater Petals and Colors

The Tibetan Master gives the colors of each petal of the human Chalice.[1]

The knowledge petals are

— orange, green, violet

— orange, rose, blue

— orange, yellow, indigo

The love petals are

---

1. Alice A. Bailey, A Treatise on Cosmic Fire (New York: Lucis Publishing Co., 1977), p. 822.

— rose, orange, green, violet

— rose, rose, orange, blue

— rose, orange, yellow, indigo

The sacrifice petals are

— yellow, orange, green, violet, rose

— yellow, orange, violet, rose, blue

— yellow, orange, rose, blue, indigo

The petals of the bud are

— pure lemon yellow with shades of white

The purer the colors of the petals and the more translucent they are, the more light, love, and power they transmit to you from Space.

The colors are related to your physical, emotional, and mental centers. Certain tones or hues in the colors are related to your etheric centers. Other tones of colors are related to your emotional and mental centers.

It is the colors of the petals that link you with the Seven Rays. Up to the Third Initiation, the petals are used, among other things, for creative imagination and visualization and for the reception of interplanetary and solar messages and energies.

In higher spheres we do not have human form but appear as Chalices or Lotuses floating and moving in Space. The colors of our Chalice prepare our future bodies, personality, and soul to act under corresponding Rays.

If your Chalice is not developing, you lose contact with the Seven Rays and cannot create balance in your whole system. The petals are related to your thoughts, feelings, and actions.

Thoughts, feelings, and actions in harmony with light, love, and sacrifice help the Chalice to grow. But we can also destroy our Chalice by using our knowledge to harm people or by living a life which is against the law of love and sacrifice. When the petals of the Chalice droop or dry, the related chakras, glands, and organs in the body lose their source of energy and fall into painful conditions.

A person who uses his knowledge to destroy people will incarnate without a healthy brain. A person who violates the law of love will be born without a healthy heart. A person who violates the law of sacrifice will have unending problems in his sex life, kidneys, and circulatory system. Any faculty that is misused is taken away from us by Nature.

Building the Chalice means to build our health, happiness, prosperity, and beauty. A human being is a reflection of the Chalice. In certain lives we may build the Chalice. In other lives we may destroy it with our harmful acts, negative emotions, vanity, ego, greed, and separatism. But eventually we learn our lessons and once again engage in the labor of building our Sacred Temple.

Some leaders think that conquering other nations and killing people are victories. But let them wait until they pass away. They will be horrified to see the conditions in which they will live when in the Subtle World.[2]

---

2. See also *Other Worlds.*

Nature continuously grinds us and gives us a chance to begin again and again until wisdom is developed.

The more you truly exist, the less karma you create. The less you exist, the more karma you create. Karma is created when your Chalice is not built or is damaged or hit by the frost of your harmful deeds.

When we speak about people being conscious or unconscious, we have a different meaning than what people ordinarily understand. A conscious person is one who is concerned about the divinity within him and the divinity in others. He is conscious that the divinity in him and in others is one with the divinity in the Cosmic Whole.

An unconscious person, no matter how cleverly he acts, no matter how much knowledge or position he holds, is ignorant, and all that he does eventually will fall upon his head. You can see this all over the world in individuals as well as in small or large nations, governments, and even empires. Unconsciousness is self-destructive and builds heavy karma.

As individuals have their Chalices, so too nations and humanity as a whole have their Chalices.

The Chalice of humanity has twelve petals exactly as that of human beings. Although these petals have different names, esoterically they are the same.

The three knowledge petals are called

— petal of civilization

— petal of culture

— petal of illumination

The three love petals are called

— petal of cooperation

— petal of loving understanding

— petal of group love

The three sacrifice petals are called

— petal of participation with the Hierarchical Plan

— petal of Purpose existing behind the Plan

— petal of precipitation — actualization of the Plan

Humanity, age after age, will be able to unfold its petals. Imagine what will happen when the whole race unfolds its nine petals. That will be the day of global Illumination.

Those who are alert and awake can see how many ages of striving, pain, and suffering are needed for humanity to reach a synthesis.

Some groups of nations represent certain petals, and as the petals unfold, we see the increase of integration and unity of nations.

The Sun represents the source of life in our solar system. This life increases its flow into humanity as the first three knowledge petals begin to unfold. It is during this process that the Law of the Solar Light permeates into the human aura. When the next three, or the love petals, open, the Love of the Solar Heart penetrates into humanity. When the next three petals, the sacrifice petals, unfold, the Life of the Central Sun reaches into the human soul and man literally becomes a child of the Sun.

What do the colors mean? Each color is the expression of a particular note which puts the petal in contact with the corresponding notes and colors of all the planes. Those who know the language of color are able to read Nature. And those who are able to read the predominating colors of a person or nation will reach definite conclusions about the development of that person or nation. They are able to see the currents of forces and energies acting in the world. They can see the harmony and the coming conflicts. Those who know how to read the language of colors know the future because Nature talks through colors.

41 | How the Petals Open

The knowledge petals open when you gradually accumulate knowledge on the physical, emotional, and mental planes. This means knowledge related to the physical world and knowledge related to the astral and mental worlds. Astral knowledge is accumulated in the astral knowledge petal. Mental knowledge is accumulated in the mental knowledge petal. All our true experiences on these planes are knowledge which nourishes the petals and makes them grow.

Falsehood does not enter into the Chalice, but it does cloud the mental plane by forming illusions. Illusions are crystallized thoughtforms accumulated in the mental plane. They make it difficult for the human soul to have access to the Chalice. They prevent clear thinking. Superstitions and prejudices are part of our illusions. Only pure knowledge enters the Chalice and accumulates there age after age.

The love petal unfolds on the physical plane through physical love, which is not always sex but may also be actions originated by love. Any action supported by love makes the love petal on the physical level open. All such love experiences are used as nourishment for the love petals.

The love petal on the emotional plane begins to unfold and grow through sincere and pure human love. Love for husband and wife, love for parents and children, love for relatives and friends all help the love petal to grow. Love for a Teacher has a very powerful affect on the emotional plane love petal.

This is why the Teaching warns us not to fall into hatred, separatism, slander, or treason but to increase our sacrificial love. Every time we fall short in our love, we bring great damage to our love petals which control certain centers in the astral and physical bodies and hurt them deeply.

The love petal on the mental plane grows and unfolds through devotion, aspiration, and dedication to plans, goals, ideals, visions, principles, and to high standards.

Fanaticism and bigotry freeze the growth of love petals because they breed hatred, jealousy, revenge, and other dark emotions.

The sacrifice petal grows and develops and radiates its fragrance on the physical plane through sacrificial actions. Every act originated by the spirit of sacrifice nourishes these petals — even a penny given in the spirit of sacrifice, or even a cup of water to a thirsty one. Great humanitarians develop their sacrifice petals easily and enjoy the joy and bliss that these petals give to their physical system. Sacrifice petals have a high degree of healing energy.

The sacrifice petal also grows on the physical plane through acts of sacrifice to clean and purify the planet, to protect the plant and animal kingdoms, and to protect nations or races that are under suppression, totalitarianism, or in danger of genocide or extinction.

We understand the beauty and value of our human mechanism on any level when we use it in the right way and cooperate with its unfoldment and growth.

The sacrifice petal on the emotional plane grows and unfolds as a result of sacrificial devotion to the human welfare. Those who sacrifice themselves to bring peace, cooperation, and harmony into the world, those who sacrifice their time, energy, money, and life to create right human relations naturally help the growth of their sacrifice petals.

Thus, all who help the human family, all who lead humanity into better relations with all the kingdoms of Nature have beautifully unfolded petals of sacrifice.

The sacrifice petal on the mental plane grows and unfolds when a person sacrifices his life for the Cosmic Laws, principles, and standards in order to bring abundance, right human relationships, illumination, and actualization of the Divine Will on earth. The sacrifice petal on the mental plane is very aromatic and has the substance of bliss, which makes the sacrificially dedicated person not only healthy and happy but also highly joyful, enthusiastic, and an untiring warrior for life.

If you read about the lives of great martyrs, you will find evidence of a great joy. This enables them to move multitudes from darkness to light, evidence of an endurance beyond human imagination. Bliss manifests as patience and endurance despite all conditions to the contrary.

The bud petals of a pure lemon color nourish the human soul, the Jewel in the Lotus, and increase its fire and glory as the nine petals develop, unfold, and radiate. As the fire of the outer petals increases, the bud petals unfold and let the fire of the human soul blaze. At this time we are told that, with the help of a watching Teacher, the human soul is released and the petals are totally burned away.

Now the Monad is an emancipated human soul, full of intelligence, love, and willpower. All his experiences are assimilated in his nature, and he leaves the mental plane and moves into the Intuitional Plane, eventually to center himself in the Spiritual Triad. Such souls are called Arhats or Warriors.

There is nothing that acts without affecting all the Universe. Nothing happens anywhere without affecting us. There is One Life. Any pressure on any part of the One Life affects the whole, the One Life. If this principle were understood and scientifically formulated and applied in our life, we would be living as superhuman beings instead of living as dwarfs.

Every word we speak is broadcast by our etheric body into the etheric body of the planet. The planetary etheric body amplifies it one thousand times and passes it into the etheric body of the solar system. Our words may be out of audible range for our hearing, but in Space there are those who hear it, record it, and if necessary broadcast it. Do not be surprised if some people meet you in the supermundane worlds and tell you they were recording your words, conversations, or lectures.

42 | The Permanent Atoms and the Chalice

We are told that each permanent atom has seven spirillae, except the mental unit which has only four spirillae. These spirillae are not always active. Some spirillae of the permanent atoms sleep for a long time until they are activated by the expansion of consciousness. The more spirillae that become active, the more the human soul enters into greater enlightenment and creativity.

The Lotus petals in the higher mental plane have a very close connection with the spirillae of the permanent atoms. For example, when the knowledge petals open fully, they help the first three spirillae of the physical permanent atom to function, and as they function they transmit more vitality to the physical body.

Similarly, when the love petals open, they affect the astral permanent atom and assist the first three spirillae in the astral permanent atom to be active.

The four spirillae of the mental unit become fully active when the seventh petal of the Lotus, which is the knowledge petal of the sacrifice petals, fully opens.

The sequence of the unfoldment of the petals does not always follow this order. They differ according to

The person's Monadic Ray

The person's karma

The person's service

It is clear that the unfoldment of petals affects the activation of the spirillae of the three permanent atoms.

The spirillae of the permanent atoms are related to the seven centers, the Seven Rays, and even to the seven sacred planets.

As the spirillae begin to function one after another, the human soul proceeds on the path of greater communication with the Universe, on the path of greater creativity and service.

The activation of the spirillae is very important because they provide health and purity to the corresponding vehicles and release the energy of the cells and atoms of the vehicles, tuning them to the Jewel in the Lotus.

Thus, the physical body becomes charged and is able to live a long and healthy life.[1]

---

1. Reprinted from *New Dimensions in Healing*, pp. 311-312.

The astral body reaches maturity and organizes itself not only to transmit magnetism and light but also to function in the Subtle World.

The mental body reaches stability and annihilates all kinds of vanity, egoism, greed, separatism, and illusions and becomes an instrument of creativity and service. The thoughts of such a mental body affect great masses of people, leading them to the path of beauty and transformation.

The expansion of consciousness, the unfoldment of the petals, and the preparation of the personality vehicles must be carried out simultaneously so that the whole man remains healthy and balanced, idealistic and realistic at the same time.

Artificial exercises and pressure upon the petals create dire consequences in the three vehicles of man.

All progress must be dealt with scientifically and without haste. A strong foundation must be laid before the structure is built.

The Lotus and Key Relationships

The Lotus relates the human soul to three centers of the planet. As it unfolds, the three permanent atoms revive and turn into sparkling lights. The disciple relates to humanity through these three permanent atoms. The physical permanent atom relates him to the physical life of humanity. The astral permanent atom relates him to the emotional life of humanity, and the Mental Permanent Atom relates him to the mental life and to the mental evolution and mental attitude of humanity. Thus these three permanent atoms relate the physical, emotional, and mental man to the corresponding spheres of humanity and keep him aware of all that is going on in these spheres.

At the beginning of this process the person feels over-whelmed by the pressure of events in the worlds and goes through various physical, emotional, and mental changes and even problems. But as the permanent atoms unfold and coordinate with each other, he finds his balance and the worldly events do not bother him very much. He develops a detached, observing attitude and intelligently responds to the needs of the world.

The petals of the Lotus relate the person to the Hierarchy. As they unfold, the person receives more impressions from the Hierarchy and regulates his life with the Plan and direction of the Hierarchy. Such impressions are unconscious until the seventh, eighth, and ninth petals start unfolding. After the ninth petal, he occasionally will have contacts with the Hierarchy or with his Master, and this will vivify all his being and bring a new vitality to his environment.

As these petals unfold, the disciple will have certain reactions. His personality limitations will react to those Hierarchical impressions which try to liberate him from his many limitations and urge him to live a more inclusive and sacrificial life and dedicate himself to the service of humanity.

As the tenth, eleventh, and twelfth petals begin to open, he starts to have conscious relations with his Master and the Hierarchy. Eventually he lives as a part of the Hierarchy. The ashramic energy charges him and manifests in his environment as a creative service in whatever field of human endeavor he is working.

When the bud or the tenth, eleventh, and twelfth petals are totally unfolded, he may have experiences of contacting Shamballa, "the Centre where the Will of God is known." Such experiences continue until the Lotus is totally burned away from the Jewel in the Lotus. It is the emancipated Jewel that contacts Shamballa, and the Arhat becomes a powerful center for the energy of Shamballa on earth.

As the permanent atoms are vivified, the petals unfold and the fire in the Chalice is released. The construction of the Antahkarana proceeds, and, after the destruction of the Chalice, the Antahkarana of the person operates between the mental unit and the Spiritual Triad.

Thus the three permanent atoms, the petals, and the Jewel in the Lotus along with the Antahkarana form one psychic device which puts the man in contact with universal values and allows him to serve with self-forgetfulness, harmlessness, and right speech.

43 | The Silvery Lotus

The Chalice has many mysteries which can be revealed as a person deepens his meditation on this subject.

There are the three tiers of petals which form the Chalice. Then we have the bud petals, which are closed around the Jewel, the human Spark. These three petals of the bud are called the Silvery Lotus. With the other nine petals, like a womb, it contains the baby, the human soul, to deliver it at the end of the Fourth Initiation.

As the Chalice unfolds and develops, all the petals become intensely luminous with translucent colors.

These petals are the womb of the Solar Angel, in which the human soul grows like an embryo.

The petals of the bud nourish the human soul with the nourishment provided through the outer nine petals and through the higher energies penetrating into the human soul.

We are told that in the Higher Worlds the Silvery Lotus appears as a bud. In the higher mental plane, the human soul appears as a Lotus, and Sages say that Space is filled with Lotuses of many colors.

The Silvery Lotus in the Chalice contains the human soul. Each soul is a Lotus.

M.M. says,

> *Therefore, he who carries the Silvery Lotus in his Chalice awakens through his vibrations the accumulations in others.*[1]

> *The harmonized currents are absorbed by the all-containing Chalice. Hence, the currents absorbed by the center of the Chalice correspond to the higher energies...*[2]

The Silvery Lotus uses the Chalice and its petals to communicate with and receive spatial fire, spatial energies, and other currents. After reception, the Silvery Lotus, the unfolding human soul, begins his process of creativity in harmony with the Cosmic Magnet. The more unfolded the Lotus, the more contact it has with the currents of the Cosmic Magnet. Hence, it is a center of right direction; it is the flower of power, the "Holy of Holies."

---

1.   Agni Yoga Society, *Infinity*, Vol. II, para. 131.
2.   *Ibid.*, para. 141.

The flower of power is the twelve-petaled Lotus. We see this symbol in Buddhism. Each Buddha is depicted sitting on a fully bloomed Lotus.

The Silvery Lotus, the three petals of the bud, slowly opens when the Initiate passes into the Fourth Initiation. Here all his psychic powers develop and are offered to the service of humanity. Arhathood is carried out on the reversed wheel of the Zodiac. During this period the Arhat spreads His beauty, glory, and creative goodness in this and Higher Worlds, whether in body or out of body.

It is during this period that the central petals gradually open and the human soul emerges slowly from the Silvery Lotus as a victorious Master.

In the *Egyptian Book of the Dead* there is a chapter called "Transformation into the Lotus." The spirit emerging from the Lotus says, "I am the pure Lotus, emerging from the Luminous Ones. ...I am the pure Lotus which comes from Solar Fields." Luminous Ones are the nine petals, from which the spirit emerges as the pure Lotus, the Innermost One.

When the petals of the Silvery Lotus begin to open, and at the moment when the human soul becomes ready to leave the Chalice, the innermost fire in the human soul destroys the Chalice and releases the Solar Angel, Itself a Lotus from Solar Fields.

People are born in a special nation or country, then become citizens of another country. According to the Ageless Wisdom, these activities are carried out under the influence of the unfolding Chalice, under the activities of the three permanent atoms of the personality, or under the influence of karma.

However, when a person begins to act under the treasury of the Chalice, he becomes a world citizen. Such people are born in any racial group or nation but actually belong to all humanity. They think, they speak, they create, and they act as if humanity were their race and the globe their own country.

It is these Chalices that eventually form parts of Global Centers. Some of them are parts of the New Group of World Servers, some are parts of the Hierarchy, and some are on the path to Shamballa. According to the unfoldment of their Chalices, they will be attracted to such Centers. Of course, they will have different duties and different responsibilities but will be involved in the task of fulfilling the same Purpose. There will be no uniformity in the colors of Chalices, except when the petals are unfolded simultaneously.

The New Group of World Servers attracts a person if his first four petals are open. Hierarchy accepts the person when eight petals are open. When the ninth petal is open, the human soul makes his first conscious contact with Shamballa. This contact continues intermittently until the petals of the bud are unfolded and the Chalice disappears in flames.

It must be mentioned here that the factors that condition the colors of the petals of the Chalice are those factors which condition the power of the natural laws, karma, and the energies interacting with the human soul.

44 | The Chalice and Centers

In the thousand-petaled Lotus we have the twelve-petaled head center, the twelve-petaled heart center, and the rest of the etheric centers.

The splenic center has its higher correspondence in the head, as all centers do. The etheric splenic center is the reservoir of prana, which passes it to the blood and regenerates the entire person.

Real healing power develops in man when the higher correspondence of the splenic center in the head begins to be active. It is through this center that an Initiate heals others, pulling energy from that center and focusing it on the patient through his eyes. This is why the look of the Initiates carries healing energy to people. This higher splenic center brings in a tremendous amount of energy from Space and focuses it through the eyes on those who are in need of that healing energy. The flow of energy is directed by an act of will operating through the eyes of the Initiate.

The twelve-petaled head center is related to the three knowledge petals of the Chalice. The twelve-petaled heart center is related to the three love petals of the Chalice. The thousand-petaled Lotus is related to the sacrificial petals of the Chalice. As the psychic energy streams down from the Core of the Chalice, it unfolds the petals of the centers and the Chalice and relates them to each other.

The fourth tier of petals of the Chalice unfolds only when total harmony and relationship is established between the petals of the head center, the higher head center,[1] the heart, and the petals of the Chalice. When this is the case, the individual disciple is entering the Fourth Initiation during which the bud will open and the Divine Spark will be a liberated human soul who will enter into the Intuitional Plane and center himself in the Spiritual Triad.

When the fifth petal of these centers and the Chalice begin to unfold and become active, this kindles the human brain. Sleeping brain centers begin to operate and make the person on the physical plane aware of higher energies, events, and currents. The coordination of these three higher centers with the petals of the Lotus slowly destroys the web which prevents a person from having conscious control on the astral plane.

It is very interesting to know that the first and second circle of petals can unfold if a person has the right relation-

---

1.   The thousand-petaled Lotus is the "higher head center."

ship with his threefold personality vehicles and with other human beings or with his Teacher, but the third circle of petals cannot be unfolded unless a person unites with an advancing group and demonstrates pure sacrificial love, dedication, and devoted service.

Many people wait many incarnations to be able to be a part of a group and demonstrate selfless and sacrificial relationships and labor. It is the group's fire that helps the individual unfold his third circle of petals. This is why group work is very important. It is in group labor that our true character comes out and passes through critical tests.

The Chalice is the symbol of a group. In the future, a group will be organized as a Lotus with twelve divisions in four groupings. Such a formation will be done scientifically with clairvoyant help so that no immature person penetrates into the group. The central fire will be the Teacher in the group who will try to help petals unfold, demonstrating service in the fields of knowledge, love, and sacrifice.

In the Higher Worlds, those groups which are sacrificial organisms and have a high level of coordination will be accepted, and spiritual duties will be given to those groups to function as centers in greater groups. This is why group integration is a supreme goal for each group member. Those who take advantage of group members or who are engaged in slander and treason are soon aborted by the group, and their evolution is delayed for many, many incarnations.

We must remember that the knowledge petals carry within them the knowledge offered in the past solar system. It was the gift of the Third Ray. This is why in the second solar system, our present one, there is no new knowledge but only the memory of all that was given in the first solar system, whether assimilated at that time or not.

All knowledge is gained through thinking, remembering, or through Intuition. This is why meditation is an effort and labor to remember, to discover the knowledge of the past given for the physical, astral, and mental planes. This is the knowledge that can be contacted through the unfolding of the three knowledge petals of the Chalice.

Love energy is the gift of this solar system, and our supreme goal is to understand this energy in all its manifestations and forms to fulfill the supreme goal of our life in this solar system. This is why if we have everything, but not *Love,* we fail in this solar system.

Those who replace love with knowledge are the failures of this solar system. This love can be understood in its threefold power through unfolding the three love petals of the Chalice and using the Love Energy.

The energy of sacrifice is offered to individuals through the sacrifice petals of the Chalice. As they unfold and radiate, this energy of sacrifice fills our nature. This energy is the energy of the future, and those who have this energy are the real *futurists*. They live in the future visions and pave the way for humanity to see the future.

Sacrifice means the outer manifestation of inner divinity, the manifestation of divinity that exists within a person and the whole of Nature.[2]

The manifestation of divinity is always accompanied by sacrificial action, sacrificial emotion, sacrificial thought.

---

2. Note: Light coincides with the knowledge petals; Love with the love petals; Power or will with the sacrifice petals.

Thus, sacrificial acts are inspired by the idea that we are all part of One Reality, and the more we help others, the more help we receive from the One Reality. This sacrifice leads us to take responsibility for the existence, security, growth, development, and future unfoldment of all human beings.

Sacrifice is a way of living in the One Reality, for the One Reality. The best that you want for yourself you give to others, knowing that you are giving to your Greater Self.

Thus, mental sacrifice, emotional sacrifice, and physical sacrifice are the result of the manifestation of your inner divinity through all your mental, emotional, and physical activities until you become one with that inner divinity. You grow into the inner divinity by trying to manifest its beauty, light, love, and power through all your thoughts, words, feelings, and actions. This is what sacrifice means in esoteric literature.

The energy of sacrifice is related to the petals of sacrifice, numbers 7, 8, and 9. They deal with group work or with planetary, all-inclusive work. The human soul, thus charged with knowledge, love, and sacrifice, assists the Plan of the Great Life of the planet to reach His Purpose.

As the sacrifice petals open, the petals of the bud, which synthesize knowledge, love, and sacrifice, slowly release the central electrical Spark, the human soul which, through his fiery essence, destroys not only the Lotus but also the three permanent atoms and releases himself into higher spheres. He is now a Threefold Fire. Such an "individual" becomes one of the founders of the next solar system.

45 | The Chalice, Centers, and Meditation

People often ask if it is permissible to meditate on the centers to activate and unfold them.

The answer to such a question is as follows: Everyone is free to experiment the way he wants, but if he wants to be safe, he must follow the experiences of Those Who are far ahead.

According to the experiences of Great Ones, we are told that the centers or chakras open when we serve, sacrifice, and expand our consciousness. This is the natural way to achieve the initiations.

In the advanced stages on the Path, your Master can change this method, due to your readiness, and give you certain meditations and visualizations by which you can hasten the development of your chakras, followed by integration and alignment.

When such a discipline is given to a disciple, he stays under the watchful eyes of the Master. The Master helps the disciple if he is in danger of overstimulation or if he gets close to burning his fuses because of the release of too much energy.

Thus meditation and visualization techniques are used to coordinate the centers and unfold their petals. It is well known that "energy follows thought" and, as such, meditation is used to help disciples think clearly and channel their energies through their visualization. No one can offer such techniques except Masters Who have the full power of clairvoyance and see the progress of the fire or the signs of danger. To be ready for such supervision, we sometimes need many decades of meditation to purify our vehicles, and we need to serve to prove that we can be trusted for the advanced work on the centers.

Sometimes even special attention on the chakras becomes unnecessary as the disciple opens the petals through his persistent and rhythmic meditation, striving, and service.

Sometimes the Teacher lets the disciple labor and leaves him free, as long as he blooms by his self-introduced labor.

During the self-initiated efforts in meditation and discipline, the disciple eventually succeeds in unfolding the petals of his Chalice and the petals of the corresponding centers.

Each change in the centers is felt in the petals of the Chalice, and any degree of unfoldment in the Chalice reflects in the centers.

Sometimes the unfoldment of the petals of the Chalice, because of striving, aspiration, meditation, and devotion, creates certain problems in the corresponding centers and related organs due to the blocked conditions existing in the centers. This is why we are always advised to purify our three lower bodies so that the energy released from the petals does not create friction in the corresponding centers.

When the Teacher sees that the disciple is ready to take risks, He gives specific meditations which help the disciple integrate and align his centers, unfold their petals, and allow the threefold fire to circulate in his bodies. This evokes certain responses from the petals of the Chalice. Such meditations are usually related to visualization techniques through which certain energies are directed to certain centers to integrate and align them with each other and with the corresponding petals of the Chalice.

46 | Meditation and Freedom

Through meditation we eventually come in contact with the plane of Intuition. Such a contact is a major event of our life because the human soul, for the first time in his life, can pass beyond the etheric web of the physical plane. If he continues his contact with the Intuitional Plane through his regular and persistent meditation and penetrates into the sixth level of the Intuitional Plane, he becomes able to pass beyond his astral body.

The freedom of the human soul from the personality vehicles will continue when he penetrates with his consciousness into the fifth sub-plane of the Intuitional Plane using the Mental Permanent Atom. At this achievement, while in the physical body, he is capable of leaving his personality and being active in the Chalice beyond the physical, emotional, and mental bodies. This is accomplished with intense aspiration, striving, service, and specifically through meditation.

It is in the Fourth Initiation that the human consciousness finally functions in the Intuitional Plane and thus destroys the etheric barrier existing on the fourth level of his mental plane.

The Tibetan Master says that at the Seventh Initiation, the man passes beyond the solar ring-pass-not.

The Chalice is not really rooted only in the higher mind. It can function outside of man; it is free in Space. When the man escapes from the etheric and astral ring-pass-nots, he functions in the Chalice and reaches a relative state of freedom. At the Third Initiation, man breaks the mental ring-pass-not, and at the Fourth Initiation the mental body is conquered and the human soul is ready now to leave the Chalice, transport its treasures into the Spiritual Triad and head center, and locate himself within the Intuitional Plane.

The Spiritual Triad is completed at the Fifth and Sixth Initiations.

Meditation thus attracts treasures into the Chalice and builds the path of freedom for the human soul.

Let us not forget that the Chalice is the anchorage point of the Solar Angel. In the Chalice, the conception and development of the human soul takes place.

We must remember that man essentially is a Monad, a ray projected out of the Central Spiritual Sun. The Monad is not the human soul. It is in the Chalice that out of this ray a human soul is conceived which then develops mind, love, and will power within an identity or individuality.

As the pearl is formed in the oyster, so the human soul is formed in the Chalice.

This ray, the Monad, connecting itself with the physical, emotional, and mental planes, eventually acts as a controlling and guiding center for these lives by which the three bodies are built. Gradually the Monad develops sentience and then thinking and acts as if It were a separate entity.

In essence ". . .the spiritual Monad is One, Universal, Boundless and Impartite, whose rays, nevertheless, form what we, in our ignorance, call the 'Individual Monads' of men. . . ."[1]

The human soul is created individually in the Lotus out of this "Boundless Ray."

The millions of personalities that are created throughout the incarnations of this individuality are like pearl beads on the thread — the ray of the Monad.

Through meditation we slowly dispel our identification with matter and gain freedom from the Cosmic Physical Plane at the time of our Seventh Initiation.

The journey is long.

This is why the Ageless Wisdom tells us that we must be souls in order to have individual consciousness, individual life, continuity of consciousness, and individual existence. We must be souls to be of assistance to the Law of Evolution on gradually higher and higher levels.

Until we build our human soul, we are an unconscious human Monad around which our past deeds, emotions, and thoughts will build a new personality in each

---

1. H.P. Blavatsky, *The Secret Doctrine*, 2 vols. (Pasadena: Theosophical University Press, 1988), Vol. I, pp. 177-178.

incarnation without having continuity of consciousness from life to life.

47 | The Jewel and the Human Soul

There is a very interesting relationship between the tiers of petals, the human soul, the Solar Angel, and the Monad.

As the knowledge petals unfold, the human soul slowly comes into being.

As the love petals unfold, they bring a greater flow of energy from the Solar Angel to the human soul.

As the sacrifice petals unfold, the human soul feels his monadic Core and receives energy not only from the Monad — his Core — but also from the inner fiery essence of the Lotus, which is electric fire. Thus, the human soul is electrified by the three-fold electrical energy — fire by friction, solar fire, and spiritual electric fire —

until his central Core is revealed and the Chalice is dissolved by the fire.

The advancing human soul, when all the petals are open, enters the path of release and steps into the Spiritual Triad. It is here that his inner diamond shines forth through the Spiritual Triad as intelligence, as pure love, and as pure willpower in harmony with the Monadic and Divine Will.

We are told that all atoms of the petals and all tiers of the petals revolve around the hidden Jewel, but when the fourth tier of petals — numbers 10, 11, and 12 — begin to unfold, they revolve in the contrary direction. As the fire of the Jewel is released, a unique beauty never dreamed of by human beings is created.

We are told that the Jewel does not revolve but rhythmically radiates eight streams of energy which reach the periphery of the four love petals and the four sacrifice petals. The Tibetan Master says that these eight rays present the eight-fold energy of atma-buddhi.

As the radiation goes on, knowledge is replaced by divine wisdom, love is absorbed in Intuition, and with the release of sacrifice all is absorbed in the central Jewel.

Before the final release of the Central Fire, the Jewel appears as seven stars within one Jewel — which is eventually absorbed into the Monad.

Thus, the human soul reaches its Fatherhood, its completion, with all its accumulations, experiences, and wisdom.

The true creativity in man starts when he is truly inspired. Such a true inspiration is not easy to achieve. We are told that in order to be inspired and to become truly creative, our monadic energy, focused in the Monad, must reach through our nine Lotus petals and through the

Golden Bridge to the physical plane. When this is a fact, then we are told that a person becomes truly creative because he is constantly in currents of higher inspiration.

48 | The Bridge

The first and major indication that the petals of the Chalice are unfolding and expanding is an increasing sense of responsibility. Then the conditions of life will improve and change as more and more people open their flower.

The sense of responsibility begins and then increases when a person starts to unfold his petals. He realizes that he is connected by invisible energy currents to the great Lives of Space and that he lives in Their Presence.[1]

The Tibetan Master says that when the sacrifice petals unfold,

---

1. For a detailed study of responsibility, please refer to *The Sense of Responsibility in Society*.

*The sacred sacrificial aspect of life is
revealed in its beauty, purity, simplicity
and in its revolutionising quality.*[2]

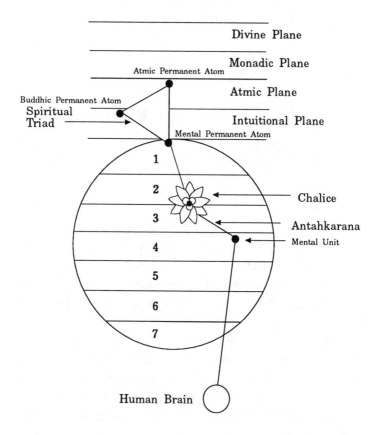

Diagram 48-1   The Bridge

2.   Alice A. Bailey, *The Rays and the Initiations* (New York: Lucis
Publishing Co., 1976), p. 31.

The Antahkarana, or the thread which gives us continuity of consciousness, connects the mental unit with the center of the Lotus and extends to the Mental Permanent Atom. The construction of this bridge of communication starts with the unfolding of the first petal and reaches completion when the nine petals of the Lotus are fully developed.

Man, living in physical incarnation, finds access into the Mental Permanent Atom and the Spiritual Triad through the Chalice.

We are told that it takes seven hundred incarnations to develop the knowledge petals; seventy incarnations are needed to unfold the love petals; seven incarnations are needed to unfold the sacrifice petals. These last seven incarnations are processes of initiation until the Transfiguration is achieved. To learn how to be sacrificial is very important; it is the major lesson that we learn to prepare ourselves for future sacrificial responsibilities.

After we become perfect human beings, we will begin to discipline ourselves to be the Solar Angels of the newly individualized animals. You can imagine how much patience, endurance, positiveness, and joy we must have to be the guardians of infant humanity.

The manifestation of your divinity on the threefold planes is accomplished through the unfolding petals of the Chalice. Throughout ages the unfolding process must go on, building better and better communication lines between your lower vehicles and between them and Higher Worlds.

It is in the furnace of the Chalice that the human soul is born. This birth process started from the date of individualization, which occurred 18,000,000 years ago, and will reach culmination when the twelve petals unfold and let the baby-god free.

H. P. Blavatsky says, "Each human being is an incarnation of God. . . ."[3]

She also says that man is the Monad.[4]

Contact with Universal Values

The opening of the petals of the Lotus is affected by the Ray of the Monad. If the Ray of the Monad is First Ray, then the third petal of each tier has an easier chance to open than the rest. The same is true for the other Rays.

However, if the bodies in which the tiers are located have a different Ray than the Monad, then friction comes into being and delays the unfoldment of the petals, until the Monadic Ray at the Third Initiation eliminates the resistance of the Ray of the bodies.

The unfoldment of the petals is not sequential. When we say that the tiers open, it is not really that simple. When the first tier opens normally to fifty percent, the second tier begins to open ten to fifteen percent, and so on. The percentage of opening of the petals is relative to each other. When the third tier of the Lotus opens sixty percent, the bud begins to open — but of course, subject to Ray influences.

Those who are First Ray Monads destroy the Chalice easily. Those who are Second Ray Monads suffer long to destroy the Chalice and be released.

---

3. H.P. Blavatsky, *The Secret Doctrine*, 3rd and rev. ed. in 3 vols. (London: Theosophical Publishing Society, 1893),Vol. III, p. 449.
4. *Ibid.*, Vol. II, p. 196.

The fourth tier of petals are called the *bud*. People think that the petals are only limited to the mental plane around the Chalice. But this is not the case. The petals start in the Chalice but slowly — as they unfold — penetrate into the corresponding bodies — etheric, astral, and mental.

Each tier expands to one plane. For example, in the etheric body you can see knowledge petals, love petals, and sacrifice petals of each tier, but the first tier predominates or is focused in the etheric plane.

Then the second tier predominates into the astral plane — with its knowledge, love, and sacrifice petals. Then the third tier is focused in the mental plane.

It is the resonance of the corresponding petals that does the job of coordination, integration, and alignment of the bodies and creating that which we call the personality.

A real personality starts between the first tier and the second tier, but still such a personality is not safe as it can change from right to left.

It is the opening of the third tier that creates the real personality which is ready now for Soul-infusion. In reality, Soul-infusion starts with the first petals.

Thus, the Soul infuses the physical, emotional, and mental bodies gradually, but when all nine petals have penetrated into the three bodies, then the personality is almost Soul-infused. Soul infusion depends upon the service of the personality, plus the unfolding petals.

49 | The Chariot

In ancient literature the Chalice was also called the Chariot which was used in wars. For example, the Lord Agni gave a war Chariot to Arjuna. Krishna and Arjuna were standing in that Chariot between two huge armies ready to attack each other. It was through that Chariot that the battle of Life was won.

The Chariot signified the Chalice, and the horses were the three knowledge petals. Arjuna was the love petals, and Krishna represented the sacrifice petals. Victory was inevitable since the Chalice was in bloom, and it was only through that fiery battle that the bud petals of the Chalice could release the ultimate victory, the release of the Divine Fire contained in the Chalice.

The process of building the Chalice is the preparation for war, which esoterically means involvement in all those activities which bring Beauty, Goodness, Righteousness,

Joy, and Freedom to humanity. The victory of those who have the Chariot given by the Lord of Fire is inevitable.

Each warrior of the Chalice or Lotus has nine powers, and these correspond to the nine petals through which ugliness, evil, unrighteousness, slavery, and gloom must be annihilated from all over the world. This is the battle of Light against darkness, and all living beings are waiting for the victory of Light.

The world will be emancipated from the dominance of every form of slavery, pain and suffering, ignorance, ugliness, and darkness only by those who build their Chalice and make themselves ready to fight for the emancipation of humanity.

It is interesting that the Chalice is built by Agni or fiery substance. We are told that the mental body is a fiery sphere in a fiery ocean. Each pure thought is a fiery arrow used to spread light, love, and sacrificial energy and cause release and breakthroughs in all fields of human endeavor, thus destroying all that is standing against light, love, compassion, and divine law.

Building our Chalice is the preparation for warriorship. It is a war in which we use all the weapons which are built within us to spread light, love, beauty, and find freedom.

Humanity has not yet understood the power of Spirit, has not understood that the final victory belongs to those who, in a real and pure sense, are spiritual on an ever progressive Path of Perfection.

Wars carried out for material gain, for self-interest, for destruction are wars that lead to defeat. Wars that are carried out for the emancipation of the One Self lead to progressive victory.

All real wars are carried out within the Lotus, the Chalice, the Chariot, because no power can stand the fire existing in the Chalice.

It is very interesting that as the physical plane warriors use their chariots in war, the spiritual warriors use their Lotus in the subtle realms. For example, all Buddhas and great Beings in the *Lotus Sutra* travel and communicate with each other sitting on lotus flowers in full bloom. These are very significant symbols. The full-bloomed Lotus releases a fire which is nothing else but a Buddha. A Buddha is a released Jewel from the Heart of the Lotus.

All heavenly wars are carried out from within the Lotus. Thus the Chariots of fiery warriors in the wars of the subtle worlds are full-bloomed Lotuses in which the Enlightened One sits with all His weapons of Light, Love, and Power.

The chariot was not only built to gain victory over physical plane life but to gain victory on the astral and mental planes as well. The victories achieved on the astral and mental planes are more far reaching than victories achieved on the physical plane.

Those who complete the construction and unfoldment of the Chalice can win victories wherever the Chalice is taken. The rays of the Chalice act as arrows of Light, Love, and Power against which no hindrance can stand. Thus the bearer of the Chalice achieves continuity of consciousness in the three worlds as did Arjuna with his Chariot in the battle of *The Mahabharata*.

In the subtle worlds the Lotus contains the warrior spirit and is carried from battlefield to battlefield to prepare the path for the Army of Light. All Great Ones in the history of humanity were and are carriers of such a Chalice. Their Chariots are the protection for humanity against forces of darkness, separation, and denial. Humanity one day will carry the Chalice of the world as a gift to Life.

The Chalice is not only a treasury but also a mechanism which absorbs many storms, arrows, and lightning. The Chalice is like a huge umbrella protecting people and locations from various attacks. The more the Chalice is unfolded, the more energy it radiates and the more attacks it receives. The presence of an unfolded Chalice is a great gift in the locations it is found.

One wonders how such a Chalice, aimed at by storms, arrows, and lightning, transforms these forces into benevolent currents and reflects them out to the world.

An unfolded Chalice is the blessing in a home, in a community. People never realize how many dangers they are daily protected from because of a Chalice, because of a person who was carrying the fiery Chalice. Where revolutions, wars, and riots occur, it indicates the absence of such Chalices in those areas.

The Bearer of such a Chalice suffers, of course, but also his heart is full of bliss.

50 | Building the Inner Temple

In the Ageless Wisdom, the greatest labor that one must be engaged in is building the Inner Temple, the Chalice. The Ageless Wisdom states that if a person builds his Inner Temple, he can be trusted to build the Temple of humanity.

This Inner Temple in man is a mechanism through which the energies of the Universe are contacted and assimilated, the laws behind them are understood, and these energies are used to build a global Temple in the psyche of humanity.

The Temple in humanity will be used for a similar purpose: to contact and record and assimilate Cosmic energies, to understand the laws behind them, and to use these energies in creative ways to help humanity make solar and galactic breakthroughs.

How this Chalice is built is very interesting. The individual Chalice is built only when the individual serves humanity by building its Chalice.

The labor is divided into seven fields. We must labor

1. To increase the light in humanity through education

2. To increase right human relations among all people everywhere

3. To provide conditions for cooperation

4. To spread beauty through the arts

5. To spread freedom

6. To spread joy

7. To demonstrate sacrificial service

Through these seven fields, the servant of humanity builds the Chalice in humanity. As the Chalice of humanity takes shape, his individual Chalice develops and unfolds in his dedicated labor of light, love, and sacrifice.

The birth of the human soul takes place in the Chalice. The birth of the soul of humanity takes place in the Chalice of humanity.

Through such a labor the human being gives birth to his own divinity, gradually, in higher and higher magnitudes.

Labor in the world is carried out on five levels:

Mechanical labor

Emotional labor

Mental labor

Spiritual labor

Divine labor

Mechanical labor is done by the urges and drives of your physical needs — food, sex, shelter, etc.

In mechanical labor, it is your body that works to meet your basic needs of life.

Emotional labor is carried out to satisfy your feelings, desires, and wishes.

Worship and devotion are parts of this labor which sublimate and eventually transform your nature, refining your feelings and emotions.

Mental labor is the accumulation of knowledge, the creative and benevolent use of knowledge, the thinking process, discrimination, analysis, and appropriation.

Spiritual labor is to conceive and give birth to your soul, to exist as a soul, and to work to manifest the *Plan* on earth.

On a higher scale, *divine labor* is to exist as a liberated Soul, to cooperate with the *Purpose* of Shamballa, to manifest your divine potential, and to work as a Master.

In spiritual and divine labor, the group members are subjectively in contact all the time with the Cosmic Magnet, with the Purpose of life, with the Plan that translates the Purpose in terms of human life, with the Masters who formulate the Plan, and with all those who consciously are working for the redemption of humanity as a whole.

Labor is carried out under seven laws. The higher the labor is, the more closely these laws are observed.

1. The law of concentration or consecration

2. The law of persistence

3. The law of obedience to the demand and need

4. The law of detachment

5. The law of economy

6. The law of discernment

7. The law of synthesis

1. Whatever you do, it must be done with all your attention and devotion — as if you were offering your service to the Most High.

2. Your labor must not depend on your mood, emotions, and personal considerations, but it must be regular and persistent, without a break in the labor.

3. You must have the spirit to obey your own highest direction, the direction of your superior, and the needs and demands of the higher nature of people.

4. Labor must be done with a detached attitude. The result must not control you. The blowing winds of emotions and opinions must not affect you. To

be detached means to be shielded from distracting, misdirecting influences.

5. You must not waste a drop of any element given to you: time, energy, money, matter, space. You must work for "the most essential" and use every drop of your energy purposefully and goalfittingly.

6. You must have a developed sense of discrimination and discernment. You are challenged to use your Intuition to do the right work, at the right time, in the right place, with the right people and the right elements. Without discernment, you waste time, energy, matter, and space and become a debtor to the karmic laws.

7. In all your labor you have the aim to work for synthesis, to build universal synthesis in all the fields of your labor.

Thus the Chalice of humanity is built petal by petal, radiating the energies of cooperation, understanding, peace, freedom, and striving toward greater achievements.

Our individual Chalices are the result of the labor we offer to build the mighty Chalice of humanity.

51 | The Birth of the Lotus

In the formation of the human Lotus, the Solar Angel, lunar pitris, and man work in cooperation. As the human being expands his consciousness, he begins to coordinate the three permanent atoms located at the base of the Lotus and builds communication lines with the physical plane.

These three permanent atoms are the physical permanent atom, the emotional permanent atom, and the mental unit, which is often called a permanent atom.

The building of the Chalice is a very mysterious process. The Chalice has four major component parts:

1. The Jewel in the Chalice

2. The bud, or bud petals

3. The petals of the three tiers

4. The Solar Angel

The three waves of the Solar Angels offered Their substance to form three petals of the bud to create with Their pressure the Diamond or the Jewel — as a compressed Space — bringing it into existence as the first step of Individuality from Homogeneity.

The three tiers of petals are built of deva substance:

1. First tier of petals   knowledge   etheric

2. Second tier of petals   love   astral

3. Third tier of petals   sacrifice   mental

Each tier has a knowledge, love, and sacrifice petal. The third tier is called also the "innermost" petals.

We have also the fourth tier which the Tibetan master calls the "bud" — the three petals which hide the "Jewel in the Lotus."

The Jewel is the Monad, the Spark, the electrical fire, or the will energy. Remember that "man is the Monad."

The substance of the bud is offered by the Solar Angel.

The petals are built of deva substance, but the unfoldment of the Chalice is due to the Jewel, to the release of the Jewel, which makes the petals open according to the unfoldment of the Jewel and eventually destroy the whole Chalice when it is fully open.

It is the Spark, the human soul, "conceived" in the Chalice that eventually is "born again" at the Fourth Initiation. Such souls are called Arhats. This is the true "second birth."

The Chalice is the womb and the body of the Solar Angel Who uses the Chalice to create a human soul out of the Monad.

The Monad is in its essence "a ray — a breath of the absolute," says *The Secret Doctrine*. It is this essence in the womb of the Chalice that is in process of metamorphosis — to turn into a human soul. It is in the Chalice that the Monad develops intelligence, love, and willpower and eventually is born as an emancipated human soul. It is at this time that the Solar Angel leaves him, and the Chalice disintegrates in the higher mental plane.

The Tibetan Master speaks about Lotuses which form groups. There are seven such groups corresponding to the Seven Rays, and these groups, as they develop, form the seven centers of the Planetary Logos. As time passes, these seven groups are synthesized into three groups in the head, ajna, and heart centers of the Logos and eventually are again synthesized in the head center of the Planetary Logos.

We can see how important is each Lotus which eventually will form a jewel in the crown of the Planetary Logos.

Each progress of the Lotus is sensed by the Planetary Logos as each labor unfolds and manifests as group consciousness, group cooperation, and group will. Each Lotus travels a long path in forming parts of the various centers of the Planetary Logos until it is finally synthesized in His head center.

Group Lotuses, which in their aggregate form a center in the body of the Planetary Logos, are cyclically stimulated, as the Planetary Logos takes Initiation or in certain times uses a given center. All Lotuses in that center are highly affected and stimulated.

If certain groups of Lotuses show inertia, glamors, and illusions, their personalities become the causes of social disturbances due to the Logoic stimulation.

Logoic centers are stimulated when

1. The Planetary Logos is visited by various Rays or Beings

2. When He takes certain Initiations

3. When He contacts certain other Logoi

4. When a certain petal of His Lotus is in process of unfoldment

5. When He establishes higher contact with His "Solar Angel"

In such cases all Lotuses related to His particular Center are affected or conquered.

Civilizations and cultures are the *responses* of group Lotuses to the impulses coming from the Core of the Planetary Logos.

The destruction, degeneration, and corruption in the world are the *reaction* of these groups to the same impulses of the Planetary Logos.

Through all these processes, we see how each individual Lotus develops group consciousness and slowly fuses its will to the will of the group Lotus.

This is why all separation and selfish activities in the world delay this process and cause pain and suffering to the incarnating human soul for thousands of years until he realizes that the goal of life is fusion and the development of group consciousness.

When the human soul reaches a certain degree of maturity in the Lotus, he begins to be aware of the petals of the Lotus — which are in essence the radiation of the threefold Monadic Life. It is in this stage that the human soul begins to cooperate consciously with the lunar pitris.

When the outer petals develop, there is a certain degree of vibratory power. This radiation reaches the three permanent atoms and vivifies the three lower spirals of the three permanent atoms. The fourth spiral is not yet vivified but affected to a certain degree.

In each Round, one of the spirals comes into being, and when the four spirals are unfolded, the human kingdom comes into being. Thus we say that the formation of the egoic Lotus began with the first Chain, developing through the second, third, and fourth Chains.

Also in the first globe of our Chain, the second and third, and in the fourth globe and Round, and in the fourth Chain, the human beings were individualized.[1]

It is very interesting to read in the Teaching of the Tibetan Master that individualization occurred at the time between the Third and Fourth Race.

The human beings who were individualized in former Chains, for example in the fourth globe of the second or third Chain, are still with us. Their permanent atoms are active now in their fifth spiral, and they are leading human beings in all fields of human endeavor.

The fire of the human soul organizes the permanent atoms and unfolds the spirals. Then the human soul consciously begins to develop the petals of the Lotus and

---

1. For additional information on Chains and Rounds, please see *Cosmos in Man* and *Other Worlds*.

begins to focus his interest on his Monadic or Divine Essence instead of his three bodies of activity. This shifting from permanent atoms to petals takes a long time during which the fire of the human soul gets stronger and stronger.

When the Solar Angels came in contact with the substance of the higher mental plane of the human being, an appearance of a fivefold vibration came into existence. This fivefold vibration evoked a fourfold vibration from the lower mind — from the subplanes seven, six, five, and four. Thus the whole mental body was organized and developed by the contact with the Solar Angels. These Solar Angels came in contact with the higher mental plane by a "driving external force."

Solar Angels have a fivefold vibration because each Solar Angel is characterized by five Rays. Their nature is formed by the combination of the Fourth, Fifth, Sixth, and Seventh Rays, and their synthesis in the Third Ray.

This fivefold vibration, combined with the fourfold vibration of the lower mind, makes a ninefold vibration established on the higher mental plane. This ninefold vibration, which is in reality nine currents of energy, circulates in the higher mental plane and gradually forms an energy whirlpool or vortex.

Each of these currents of energy gradually fuse with the fiery petals of the bud.

The Tibetan Master says that the petals are like "vibrant and scintillating lights." After the bud was formed, a triangle of energy appeared and circulated between the Mental Permanent Atom, the center of the bud, and the mental unit found on the fourth subplane of the mental body. This triangle, says the Tibetan Master, was formed "of pure electrical manasic fire."[2] It is this triangle that eventually will be the foundation of the Antahkarana.

From this point on begins man's great labor to build a bridge between these three points — the mental unit, the Mental Permanent Atom, and the center of the Lotus — with his own labor, sacrifice, and service to win by his own hands and feet the right of his own existence, his individuality.

This fiery triangle is used as an electrical line to transmit intuitional light to the center of the Lotus, creating the three bud petals "which close in on the central flame."

This Lotus is the womb in which the human soul is in gestation. The fire in the Lotus is the fire of the spirit which will substantiate as a human soul and take birth through the fire at the Fourth Initiation. It is at that time that man will be a living *soul* ready then to step on the path of mastery and say, "Be courageous. I conquered the world."

The triangle formed by the Mental Permanent Atom, the center of the Lotus, and the mental unit slowly disappears, and the fire that was circulating through the triangle is focused within the Lotus.

The formation of the Lotus, in actuality, is the construction of a powerful magnet on the mental plane to draw the energy of the Monad, the energy of the ray of Spirit, and anchor it in the center of the Lotus. This is the moment of conception in the mental womb, the Lotus. The focus of Spirit in the Lotus is the Jewel, the future

---

2.   Alice A. Bailey, *A Treatise on Cosmic Fire*, p. 709.

human soul and individualized Self, the Son of God on earth.

Thus the Jewel is within the twelve-petaled Lotus to form, to grow, to unfold, and one day to release himself and take a glorious birth. This Jewel throughout ages and through many incarnations is impressed by the Solar Angel with the Purpose, the Home, and the Plan. These are his heavenly food. As the Jewel in the Lotus awakens, he remembers these instructions, feels the purpose of life, and begins to live a life that is in harmony with the Laws of the Higher Worlds.

The unfoldment of the Lotus is responsible for the change in the chemistry of our body. Even the genes and DNA are changed by the unfolding Lotus. The immediate effect of the unfolding Lotus is upon the mental, astral, and etheric centers and upon our thoughts, emotions, and actions.

Chemists and other health professionals try very hard to convince us that all the components of our health — our glands, etc. — are the result of our genes. This may be true, but they cannot explain the cause of the special chemistry of the genes.

The Ageless Wisdom says that it is our past thoughts, words, and actions that produce the special genes we have. The recordings of the genes are the summary of the recordings of our permanent atoms — which are permanent recorders of our life in the three worlds. Certain thoughts, certain emotions, and certain actions are related to certain chemicals in our body. Let us remember that thoughts, emotions, and actions are themselves chemicals which the person produces through using his mental, emotional, and etheric substances. It is their psychic chemistry that affects our physical chemistry through changing the composition of our genes.

Of course, the medical and health professionals will have difficulty believing that our physical chemistry is the result of our past mental, emotional, and physical actions unless they believe in the continuity of life. But they may deduce that in one life we can change the chemistry of our bodies and genes through the way we think, feel, and act.

One of the greatest responsibilities of the Solar Angel is to impart impressions about the Purpose and the Plan to the baby Jewel in the womb of the Lotus. The presentation of the Plan and Purpose to the developing human soul is carried on in the following way: The Solar Angel takes a tiny part of that Purpose and impresses the human soul with just the dosage that he can understand, assimilate, and use in his life condition. The Solar Angel transmits first a part of the Plan, and as the person's sensitivity expands more, the Solar Angel begins to transmit a tiny part of the Purpose.

For many years or for many incarnations the human soul unconsciously follows the Plan and the Purpose, though with many falterings, hesitations, and complications, until one day he consciously sees the Plan and then sees the Purpose behind the Plan.

Of course a fuller understanding of the Plan and Purpose dawns in his consciousness as he passes from initiation to initiation, and his life becomes a center for the actualization of the Plan and later of the Purpose.

It is important to note that as a person becomes more conscious of the Plan he feels more energy and a greater urge toward creativity throughout his whole system. And as he becomes more conscious of the Purpose, he synchronizes his will with the Divine Will.

One begins to be conscious of the Plan when the sixth petal of his Lotus opens. The consciousness of Purpose comes after the nine petals are fully open.

During the transmission of the Plan and Purpose to the human being and while watching over the development of the petals of the Lotus, the Solar Angel also tries to stimulate the fifth spiral of the permanent atoms. Through such a stimulation, great opportunities come on our path.

52 | The Lotus and Self-Consciousness

The Lotus is the seat of Self-consciousness. It is the mechanism which builds the pearl out of the substance of spirit, endowing it with intelligence, love, and willpower. For long eons of time, the human soul was not in existence. What existed in man was the Solar Angel. The Solar Angel was the man. But the duty of the Solar Angel is to conceive man and make him a Self-conscious being and then leave him to continue his Path of evolution on his own.

There is a relationship between the petals of the Lotus and the three permanent atoms. We are told that the knowledge petals work with the physical permanent atom. This means that whatever occurs in our physical life is passed on to the Chalice through the knowledge petals.

Of course it is those experiences that are related to Beauty, Goodness, Righteousness, Joy, Freedom, Striving, and Sacrificial Service that are passed on.

Our love petals work through the astral permanent atom, and experiences related to our emotional nature go into the Chalice.

Our sacrifice petals work with the Mental Permanent Atom, and experiences of a mental nature go into the Chalice.

On the other hand, the petals, by their purity, improve the three bodies through the permanent atoms and enable them to be sensitive toward those experiences that have value and can be collected into the Chalice. This leads the three bodies toward more and more refinement.

The petals are also related to certain centers.[1] For example, the knowledge petals are related to the generative organs in the mental body, to the throat center in the astral body, to the generative organs in the astral body, to the throat center in the etheric body, to the generative organs in the physical body.

The love petals are related to the solar plexus in the mental body, to the heart center in the astral body, to the solar plexus in the astral body, to the heart center in the etheric body, to the solar plexus in the physical body.

The sacrifice petals are related to the base of spine in the mental body, to the head center in the astral body, to the base of spine in the astral body, to the head center in the etheric body, to the base of spine in the physical body.

---

1. Remember that the Chalice has its twelve petals just as our centers in all our vehicles have their proper number of petals.

Thus you see that the petals, centers, and permanent atoms are related to each other through a network of energy lines, affecting each other in positive or negative ways.[2]

When a person is developed, any precipitation from the Chalice spreads into the three bodies bringing health, happiness, prosperity, joy, and peace.

It is very interesting to know that the central Jewel relates to the mental unit, which in its turn is related to the mental spleen, astral spleen, etheric spleen, and physical spleen. And if the Antahkarana is built, the mental unit will be related to the Mental Permanent Atom.

The petals are related also to higher planes. For example, the knowledge petals are related to the Manasic Permanent Atom and to the intelligence aspect of the Monad. The love petals are related to the Buddhic Permanent Atom and to the love-wisdom aspect of the Monad. The sacrifice petals are related to the Atmic Permanent Atom and to the will aspect of the Monad.

It is also given in the Teaching that the thread of energy reaches the Planetary and Solar Logoi.

Thus, the Lotus in man is the real heart center which relates man to the mundane and supermundane worlds.

To further clarify the relationship of the petals to the centers, we may say that as the knowledge petals unfold, the petals of the sacral center and later, the throat center, begin to open. And if the knowledge petals are opened under a certain amount of pressure, the sex (or sacral) center demonstrates violent activities for a while until the

---

2. For detailed information on the bodies and centers, please see *New Dimensions in Healing*.

petals of the center appropriate themselves to the rhythm of the knowledge petals.

As the love petals of the Chalice unfold, they create pressure on the petals of the heart center in the head to unfold parallel to the love petals of the Chalice.

The love petals of the Chalice relate a person to humanity. As the love for humanity unfolds, the person feels at one with humanity and shares its joys and sorrows and, in the meantime, turns into a stream of love that pours into the Chalice of humanity.

The petals of the heart center relate a person to a group and react to the group "unhappiness or happiness." The love petals of the Chalice open as the human being shows real concern about the condition of humanity. The joys and sorrows of humanity stimulate these petals and help them unfold. The same is true for the heart center in relation to group life. Group joys or group sufferings affect the heart center, and the person begins to transcend his personal love and feel the group love.

As the sacrifice petals unfold, they exercise pressure on the petals of the center at the base of the spine, which gradually releases the central fire to climb up the spine. When this process begins and as the bud petals of the Chalice unfold, the petals of the head center open and draw the energy of fire from the base of spine and fuse with it.

The unfolding of the sacrifice petals allows a man to enter the path of true leadership, a leadership which is carried out to unite humanity and to bring humanity under the influence of the Tower, the Will of Shamballa.

53 | Psychic Energy

Psychic energy emanates from the Core of the Lotus, and, passing through the mental, astral, and etheric centers, it unfolds their petals. The more the petals are unfolded, the more the psychic energy flows through the centers. Thus, centers are the distributors of psychic energy.[1]

Real psychism is the result of the display of psychic energy through the various centers of Initiates or Masters.

Each new flow of psychic energy expands the human consciousness. Thus consciousness is conditioned by the flow of psychic energy and by the degree of unfoldment of the petals of the centers.

---

1. See also *A Commentary on Psychic Energy* and *New Dimensions in Healing* for information on psychic energy and the etheric body and centers.

Greater consciousness is the result of a greater unfoldment of the centers.

The main flow of psychic energy originates from the Core of the Lotus, but it is "ruled" by the degree of the unfolding petals of the Lotus.

The entire network of centers on etheric, astral, and mental planes is connected with the petals of the Lotus. These petals affect each other and the flow of psychic energy.

Increasing psychic energy is the result of harmonious development of the centers in the personality vehicles and the petals of the Chalice.

Enlightenment occurs every time petals on various levels synchronize. Greater enlightenment is the result of synchronization of higher petals.

The three stages of Illumination are the result of the synchronization of three petals, five petals, and seven petals.

Those centers which have less than seven petals enter into pralaya when the others unfold their higher petals. A hint is hidden here.

After the unfoldment of the seven petals of the Lotus, the human consciousness begins to penetrate into the Intuitional Plane. Consciousness on the Intuitional Plane is called awareness.

We must remember that each stage of development of the petals affects also the spirals of the permanent atoms, which are the connecting links between vehicles. In them are stored the records of the activities of corresponding vehicles.

The Chalice is the main source of impulse. The level of the Chalice is conditioned by the degree of unfoldment of the centers and permanent atoms. The Chalice is especially affected by the recordings found in the permanent atoms.

Relationship with Higher Groups

Each tier of petals connects the human soul to the Cosmic Center because each of them came into being under the influence of the major Rays. For example, the knowledge petals are related to the Third Ray. The love petals are related to the Second Ray of Love-Wisdom. The sacrificial petals are related to the First Ray of Willpower.

As the Lotus unfolds the consciousness of man, it relates itself more closely to the spheres of the three Rays, contacts Cosmic Sources of energy and wisdom, and translates them creatively into the threefold mechanism of the human existence.

Thus the Lotus is an interconnecting link between earth and Cosmos, and, as it unfolds, the human soul realizes that he is a citizen of Cosmos.

Lotuses, starting on the third or second mental levels, form groups. They live as groups. We are told that there are seven kinds of egoic groups according to the seven Rays. All of them form a complete group but with different colors and radiations.

Each group is attracted to one of the seven centers of the seven Planetary Logoi. Each group acts as a center for our Planetary Logos.

Seven groups of Lotuses form one center in the body of our Planetary Logos. But each of these groups is related to other Planetary Logoi. Each group is a part of a specific center that the particular Planetary Logos has.

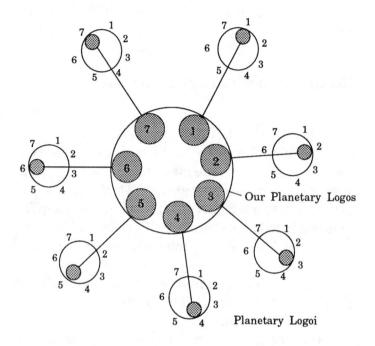

Diagram 53-1 Chalices as Centers

We must remember that each Planetary Logos has seven centers, and, with all Their centers, each of Them operates as a center in the body of the Solar Logos.

Groups of Lotuses arrange themselves according to their Ray and evolution with one of these greater Centers and become part of It.

This apparently isolated human being, through his Lotus, is related not only to other human beings but also to the planets and to the solar system and, through the Lotuses of these Logoi, to the whole Cosmos.

An interesting point is that the consciousness of the Planetary and Solar Logoi operates through these groups of Lotuses.

As the human soul unfolds, he will slowly be aware that through him the Planetary Logos, and later the Solar Logos, will work. The sense of responsibility originates from the awareness of such relationships. This is why so much emphasis is put on group work on the earth and in forming groups of various kinds dedicated to service. Each group is a training field to prepare human souls to fit themselves to higher groupings, which are groupings of Lotuses.

54 | The Chalice and the Auric Egg

In esoteric literature the auric egg and the Chalice are used synonymously. It is true that they are the same, but they are two phases of the same unit.

The auric egg is a sphere of light, having in it the potentiality or the blueprint of the Chalice.

The Chalice is the unfolding potentiality within the auric egg.

As the Core of the auric egg unfolds, a new entity comes into being within the egg. We call this entity the twelve-petalled Lotus or the Chalice, the center of which is the Spark of Life.

The auric egg is the sphere of radiation of the Solar Angel in which, as if in a womb, the human embryo takes form until he becomes a full grown soul.

This growth is seen in the unfolding petals of the seed of Life.

As the petals unfold in the transparent sphere of the auric egg, the human soul comes into existence.

When the Chalice or the Lotus is formed, the individuality of the human soul begins to form. It is this individuality that leaves the bodies during death and comes back and forms his bodies according to his past karma.[1]

Thus we know that it is the Chalice that enters the heavenly abodes — Devachan.

The Core of the Chalice is the human essence, the human Spirit. This means it is the human entity in the form of the Chalice that enters into Devachan, glorified by the light of the Solar Angel.

We are told that the substance of the auric egg essentially is given to us by the Solar Angel. This substance is mixed with the substance of the higher mind.

After the human soul leaves his lower mental body, the radiation at the center of the Chalice forms an egg-shaped aura, a translucent aura in which the Lotus appears with its colorful petals.

Some of these auras have human form, as long as the human soul still thinks in terms of being in human form, but gradually that thoughtform disappears and only the Lotus is seen.

In esoteric literature, we are told that ". . . It is the Sutratma, the silver 'thread' which incarnates, from the beginning of the Manvantara to the end, stringing upon itself the pearls of human existence [the personality], in

---

1. See also *Other Worlds*.

other words, the spiritual aroma of every personality it *follows* through the pilgrimage of life."[2]

To understand this we must remember that the Monad, which we think of as a unit and the Core of the human being, is nothing else but a *ray*. It is this ray that eventually individualizes and builds a self-hood. Until this self-hood is built, there is nothing that incarnates but the life thread, the *sutratma*, around which the physical, emotional, and mental atoms build a personality as a result of past actions, emotions, and thoughts. Until a human being becomes a conscious human soul, all life runs mechanically. There is no conscious entity that is born and dies, but all aggregations of bodies disperse and gather together again around the sutratma.

This means that after death there is no one to be conscious, and after birth there is no one to remember the life events during the period of death.

After the human soul begins to form, it is the human soul that passes away and is born, gathering around himself his lower vehicles according to his thoughts, words, feelings, and actions.

One day a Teacher explained the sutratma and human soul by taking a string and making a knot on it. The knot is the human soul, a continuation of the life thread. Man then has self-consciousness and in the meantime the awareness that he is one with the whole life energy, though this awareness comes much later.

It is after building the human soul that he will gradually understand the mysteries of manifestation and,

---

2. H.P. Blavatsky, *The Secret Doctrine*, 3rd and rev. ed. in 3 vols., Vol. III, p. 446.

stage by stage, advance in consciousness to the Central Mystery from Whom he originated.

This means if you are not individualized and have not become a living soul, there is no life after death for you because you have no continuity of consciousness. But if you are a soul and unfolded to a certain degree, you become conscious in the astral plane, and then you sleep as you go to the mental plane and come back into incarnation.

And if you are a soul and unfolded to a high degree, you go to Devachan and enjoy a long period of bliss and come back bringing great impressions of beauty, harmony, and bliss.

If you have built the Antahkarana, you even remember your life in the other worlds. This happens between the Third and Fifth Initiations.

Fortunately, most of humanity has to a certain degree developed its soul, and people have relative awareness in the subtle world. Such an awareness is the cause of suffering both in the subtle world and in the physical world.

H.P. Blavatsky says, referring to the auric egg, "It is this Body which, at death, assimilates the essence of Buddhi and Manas and becomes the vehicle of these spiritual principles, *which are not* objective, and then, with the full radiation of Atma upon it ascends as Manas-Taijasi into the devachanic state. . . ."[3]

"It is also the material from which the Adept forms his Astral Bodies [the etheric body], from the Augoides

---

3.   *Ibid.* [Taijasi means luminous, shining, irradiating — manas mixed with the light of Intuition.]

and the Mâyâvi Rûpa downwards."[4]

She continues, "After the death of man, when its most ethereal particles have drawn into themselves the spiritual principles of Buddhi and the Upper Manas [the Higher Mind] and are illuminated with the radiance of Atma, the Auric Body remains either in the Devachanic state of consciousness, or in the case of a full Adept, prefers the state of a Nirmanakaya, that is, one who has so purified his whole system that he is above even the divine illusion of a Devachani."[5]

"Thus the Auric egg, reflecting all the thoughts, words and deeds of man, is:

(a) The preserver of every Karmic record,

(b) The storehouse of all the good and evil powers of man, receiving and giving out at his will — nay, at his very thought — every potentiality, which becomes, then and there, an acting potency...

(c) As it furnishes with his Astral Form [the etheric body] around which the physical entity models itself, first as a foetus, then as a child and man."[6]

"Further, H.P.B. points out that the māyāvi-rūpa [the illusionary body], or body of thought and feeling projected by the Adept at his will, is formed of the

---

4. *Ibid.* [*Augoides* is the radiation of the human soul seen in the etheric body. *Mayavirupa* is the etheric body charged and amplified by the four Cosmic ethers.]

5. H.P. Blavatsky, *The Secret Doctrine* Vol. III, p. 446.

6. *Ibid.*, p. 495.

substances and energies of appropriate layers of the auric egg; and just because such projections of the auric substance are for temporary purposes, the māyāvi-rūpa possesses its name — 'illusionary body.' . . .It is not only the field of all the different ranges of consciousness of the embodied man, but it is likewise the ethereal, astral and even spiritual substance, or auric envelope, out of which are formed every one of the vehicles of the human entity including linga-sharira, māyāvi-rūpa, his devachanic auric shell and his kama-rupa after death."[7]

"Auric envelope or the essence of [visible] man. . . ."[8]

"Now the formation of the astral man [the etheric body] takes place within the auric egg of the ex-devachani. From the moment when the ego leaves the devachanic condition, the astral form [the etheric body] becomes steadily more complete or definite as the gestating entity approaches the entrance into the womb. The ray from the incarnating ego enters first the aura and later the womb of the mother-to-be by means of the growing astral form [the etheric body] which takes its rise in and from the most appropriate life center — or life-atom latent in the auric egg of the incoming entity."[9]

". . .Prana and the Auric Envelope are essentially the same. . . ."[10]

Alice A. Bailey says that the auric egg is "the causal body."[11]

---

7. H.P. Blavatsky, *Collected Writings*, Vol. XII, p. 647.
8. *Ibid.*, p. 563.
9. *Ibid.*, p. 649.
10. *Ibid.*, p. 694.
11. Alice A. Bailey, *Letters on Occult Meditation*, "Glossary," p. 351.

Prana and the life thread are the same. Prana and the life thread emanate from the Monad and then branch and form the essence of all vehicles.

As the Chalice unfolds its petals, the auric egg grows larger until it appears as the body of glory all around the physical man.

It is through this aura that the Initiate receives all impressions from the higher Source, and when he enters into Devachan, his aura registers all the bliss and beauty by which he is surrounded in that sphere.

But as we mentioned earlier, most of the advanced Initiates do not enter into Devachan as Their labor on earth calls Them back to earth.

55 | The Petals and Higher Service

The unfoldment of the petals of the Chalice is related to the ability of the person to communicate with Higher Initiates and even offer his bodies for service to Great Ones. For example, if five petals of the Chalice are unfolded — which means all three knowledge petals and two love petals — the disciple will be a transmitting agent of the Christ, or one of the Masters, during his "lecturing, writing, or teaching." Then the words of the disciple will reach multitudes with creative fire and inspiration, spread the intention of Christ, and help Him to create new conditions all over the world.

Imagine the power they would create if thousands of disciples with their five petals opened offered themselves to the Christ to spread His service.

Also we are told that Great Ones, Christ and His Masters, can work in a different way to help humanity. This is a little more advanced way than the previous one. If a disciple has six petals unfolded — three knowledge petals, and three love petals — he can consciously step out of his body and offer it to one of the Masters or Christ to operate through it and come in contact with the dense physical life. In the near future such disciples, male and female, will offer their bodies to great Masters, and Masters will operate through them.

As in everything, the dark lodge is also able to utilize such a method by obsessing and possessing people in various places in the world to discredit beforehand those who will be transmitters of the light, love, and power of the Great Lords.

Human beings will discern the agents of dark forces from the agents of the Forces of Light by the following signs:

1. Those who have their sixth petal unfolded will never make a claim about their personality ego but will work and demonstrate the power of energy spreading through them.

2. They will never advertise or engage in channelling, psychic reading, past life reading, or fortune telling activities. They will never talk about great Initiates possessing them and talking through them.

3. They will always speak about unity, synthesis, and inclusiveness.

4. They will never serve separative interests but will emphasize the Brotherhood of One Humanity.

5. They will create understanding between world religions and eliminate those expressions which were not uttered by Great Ones.

6. They will bring great progress to all fields of human endeavor.

7. They will establish Centers of Light all over the world through advanced disciples and aspirants.

Of course, those who will have their fifth and sixth petals unfolded will be those who have since childhood dedicated their lives to the service of humanity and have a glorious record of service in their past lives.

The human soul, the real identity of a person, can consciously vacate his body when his sixth petal is duly unfolded.

Not everyone with such an achievement offers his body to Great Ones to function through, but it occurs when the need is great and when the time demands it for a great service.

Such service will start in every country, we are told, near the year 2000 and will continue until the Christ reappears on earth. During the reappearance, all such advanced people will serve as a team in His labor.

This is why it is so important that students of the world study about the Chalice from as many angles as possible and try to unfold their petals through expansion of consciousness and through love and dedicated service to humanity.

56 | Three Processes

There are three processes which will lead us to Arhathood, to Fourth Degree Initiation. They are called

Transmutation

Transformation

Transfiguration

These processes are carried out under the power of the unfolding Chalice. The knowledge petals introduce to your physical, emotional, and mental substances the process of transmutation. As the knowledge petals unfold, you feel refinement in your physical, emotional, and mental bodies, in your actions, emotions, and thoughts. Transmutation is the process by which you change the atoms in your bodies from atoms of inertia to atoms of rhythm.

This is how our physical body becomes energetic and charged with the spirit to serve. Because of the transmutation process, inertia, depression, laziness, and apathy disappear. Anger, hate, jealousy, and revenge disappear. Fear, greed, and vanity disappear. Thus, the body, the emotional vehicle, and the mental mechanism grow beautifully, responding to the knowledge petals existing on the three personality levels. When this is the case, our physical body reflects tenderness, our emotional body reflects intuitive light, and our mental body reflects the light of the higher mind.

When our body is purified to a certain degree through the transmutation process, our health increases, our energy and dynamism increase, and our body becomes more adaptable to the changing conditions of life.

Our emotional body radiates joy, love, and peace and does not distort intuitional flashes coming from the higher planes.

As the mental body is transmuted, it becomes a clean mirror for higher visions and revelations and it develops an advanced power of creativity.

The color of our mental body turns into a pure lemon yellow light from the center of which radiate the twelve rays of a rainbow.

When the fourth petal — the first petal of the love petals — begins to unfold, it creates transformation in the human body. As the next two love petals unfold, the transformation and real integration of the personality vehicles (physical, emotional, and mental) take place.

Transmutation is the development and refinement of the atoms of your bodies.

Transformation is related to the change of the forms that are built by the transmuted atoms.

For example, we have individual diamonds transmuted from coal. Transformation occurs when these diamonds are brought together to build a diamond form: a heart, a ring, a necklace, etc.

In the same way the transmuted atoms under the power of the love petals change the form and color of your eyes, your nose, your face, your entire body.

Transformation also occurs in your astral body and mental body. Your whole personality transforms and comes closer to the archetype in the Heavenly Man. Transformation of the vehicles makes them more sensitive to the positive energies in Nature and, because of this sensitivity, they exercise a great influence on the bodies of others as well as on the bodies of the plant and animal kingdoms, thereby causing transformation in them.

Transmutation and transformation lead to the process of transfiguration.

Transfiguration is the revelation of the fire of the Inner Divinity in your body, emotions, and mind.

Transfiguration is the result of the unfolding of the sacrifice petals. Transfiguration totally ends the power of the personality over you, the human soul. Once this power is lifted, for the first time you become your True Self.

After transfiguration, there is another process which is called Freedom. This is achieved when you, the human soul, under the influence of the unfolding bud petals, transcend the personality vehicles and enter the Intuitional Plane. There you understand the meaning of true freedom, and you begin to conquer time and space.

A Fourth Degree Initiate is a Jewel living in a twelve colored rainbow.

57 | The Chalice and Healing

The healing energy is the energy of the Jewel in the Lotus.

This energy is capable of healing the physical body, the emotional body, and the mental body if man does not prevent the flow and proper circulation of this energy through his

— wrong thoughts

— wrong emotions

— wrong actions

Wrong action prevents the flow of the energy of the sacrifice petals or, if the person is in a low stage of evolution, of one of the petals of the knowledge petals.

Wrong emotional attitudes prevent the flow of energy of the love petals or of the love petal of the knowledge petals.

The energy flow from the knowledge petals is prevented through our wrong thoughts, motives, and ugly, separative intentions. It is these disturbances that prevent the healing energy from reaching our lower bodies and healing their various diseases and disturbances.

Disturbances in our nervous system are caused by our negative emotions, which block the love petals and prevent the flow of the healing energy from reaching our nervous system and related parts of the body affected by nerve, blood, and lymphatic disturbances.

Negative emotions prevent this flow of healing energy emanating from our Core. It is the love petals, not the emotional permanent atom, that let the energy reach the astral body and heal it.

In the future, advanced medicine will be able to prove this and find ways and means to make the flow of Core energy reach our vehicles. At that stage people will enjoy health and happiness in these planes of their personality.

One hundred years ago no doctor related the physical, emotional, nerve, blood, and mental problems to our thoughts, feelings, and actions.

At the present we have future oriented physicians who are looking for the deeper causes of human diseases. The recognition of psychosomatic illness was a great step forward. Medical professionals as well as other people are talking about meditation and about virtues as agents of healing.

Once the Chalice is recognized, the healing of nations will enter a new phase which will change all modern techniques.

The real power behind the petals is that each group of petals is a communication line between us and some Higher Beings.

These groups of petals, as they unfold, connect the human soul not only with the Spiritual Triad but also with heavenly Lords Who are centers of Intelligence, Love, and Willpower.

The Lotus is a connecting link between the human and the Divine, and higher psychic gifts are gifts from these great Lords to man through the link of the Lotus.

58 | Principles and the Chalice

A principle is a thread on which you hang various activities, emotions, and thoughts as beads which are supported by the principle. The Seven Rays have seven principles. Each Ray has a principle on the thread of which hang the beads of existence, lives, kingdoms, and all forms.

Each principle has its own will, its own law, according to the planes on which the principle is in operation. These wills are called

1. The Will to Initiate

2. The Will to Unify

3. The Will to Evolve

4. The Will to Harmonize and Relate

5. The Will to Act

6. The Will to Cause

7. The Will to Express

These laws function as enforcers of the will of the principle.

Each law can change its name and thus function on different levels under different names. But all these sub-laws pursue the will of the principle.

The principle is the core, is the source from which emanates all laws, conditioned and programmed in such a way that they work for the fulfillment of the will of the principle.

Every law is a carrier of power and energy. It is not wise to stand against it. It is possible to misuse a law, but the principle in the law eventually eliminates all who stand against it.

The principle in man is the Monad. The Monad has its laws. This principle functions through the bodies, and in each body the principle has a specific law.

To benefit from these principles, we give different names to them and call them, for example:

• The Principle of Freedom

• The Principle of Love

• The Principle of Light

• The Principle of Harmony, Beauty, and Cooperation

- The Principle of Enlightenment

- The Principle of Causation

- The Principle of Sharing

These principles radiate particular laws to promote the actualization of freedom, love, light, and so on. For example, the principle in politics is to create freedom. This principle can inspire various bodies to work for freedom under certain laws. All activities, techniques, ways, and means must obey the laws of the Principle of Freedom in order to actualize the will of that principle.

Human relationships are based on these seven principles. Right human relationship is the utilization of laws to actualize the principles. If any principle is violated by a man-made law, or intentionally, the violator receives a destructive shock from the will of the principle. This shock may take time to manifest as destruction on the lower planes, but it never errs. Cooperation is a principle. No matter what you think, speak, and do, it must be in harmony with the Principle of Cooperation.

People often condemn each other because of their actions, words, and thoughts. The best method to help a failing brother is not to condemn him but to bring to his attention the principle that was violated and encourage him to live for that principle.

There are also man-made principles which can serve a purpose if they are representing a real principle. For example, one may say to a group of people, "Our principle will be to have respect for each other in all possible conditions." This is a sub-principle and is in harmony with a greater principle. But another may propose, "Our principle will be to kill by any means." This is not a principle but the manifestation of an illusion, glamor, self-interest, revenge, hatred, etc.

Principles rule the world because they are energy currents. They cannot be violated. Man-made principles or rules or orders that violate the seven principles given above become self-destructive.

Those nations, groups, or individuals that live in harmony with principles last forever and, cyclically, they lead other nations into light. To live in a principle means to have with you the available energy of the source of the Rays.

You can ponder on the seven principles given above and instill them in your mind as a guiding light in your thinking, talking, and all activities.

The petals in the Chalice are in a mysterious way the representatives of the Principles of Beauty, Sacrifice, Love, and Light. As the petals open, we start understanding the significance of principles and intuitively absorb the power of the laws related to these principles.

The twelve petals represent seven white and five black notes of the piano of life. The seven notes are the living essence of the twelve petals. As the petals unfold, we demonstrate understanding of the seven principles and live according to the laws of the principles. As the petals unfold completely and are burned away by the central fire, the human soul transcends the laws and lives in harmony with the essence of the principles.

Later, on the Path of evolution when one reaches the level of Resurrection, the seven principles merge and the Resurrected One lives in the one Principle of Compassion. Compassion is one of the Cosmic principles.

Principles in the Chalice guide our steps until the Fourth Initiation. Principles in the Spiritual Triad guide us until the Seventh Initiation. After that, one prepares to leave the Cosmic Physical Plane and live in the one Law of Compassion . . . and that is a new beginning.

The galactic Chalice has its Jewel, and this Jewel is the Source of the seven galactic laws, the Cosmic Rays. The Jewel in the Lotus is the principle controlling the galactic Whole. The galactic Jewel is what we call the Cosmic Magnet.

A law is a principle on Cosmic levels. A principle is the law manifested through the planes. Our Seven Rays are seven principles, but the Source of our Seven Rays is the Cosmic Law of Compassion. Together with the Law of Compassion there are six other Cosmic laws, which make a total of seven Cosmic Laws emanating from the one galactic principle.[1]

---

1. For information on the Seven Rays, please refer to the video, *The Seven Rays Interpreted*.

59 | Time and the Chalice

The three tiers of the Chalice — made up of the knowledge, love, and sacrifice petals — correspond to the past, present, and future. The knowledge petals are related to the past. The love petals are related to the present. The sacrifice petals are related to the future.

The person lives in a concept of measurement of time during the development of these three tiers. During the opening of the first tier, all past knowledge slowly becomes available to him and the Law of Economy is understood. During the unfoldment of the love petals, existence is seen in terms of the present, and the person uses knowledge for the present. During the unfoldment of the sacrifice petals, existence is contemplated in terms of the future. Knowledge, love, the Law of Economy, and the Law of Attraction and Repulsion are brought together within the Law of Synthesis and into the principle of the future. All that is done, felt, and thought are for the future.

It is during the unfoldment of the bud petals, between the Third and Fourth Initiations, that the concept of time is transcended and the *awareness* of man begins to live in the Eternal Now. He still has knowledge, but it is a knowledge that belongs to eternity. He still has love, but it is a love that is total compassion. Still he has awareness of the meaning of sacrifice, but it is related to the Purpose and to the Will of the One Who embraces the Whole.

During the period of unfoldment of the three bud petals and after its completion, the Initiate begins to develop the power of prophecy. His awareness works in the Eternal Now, and he sees the formation of events and their precipitation in the three lower worlds. An Initiate uses the lower three permanent atoms — the physical permanent atom, the emotional or astral permanent atom, and the mental unit — to translate the progression of events in terms of physical, emotional, and mental fields. But the true Prophet begins to function when His awareness is focused on Atmic and Monadic Planes — when One is a Fifth or Sixth Degree Initiate.

Such Prophets do not involve Themselves with personality events, but They are concerned with the events related to humanity, to the globe, to the chain, and even to schemes. Prophets open the future for us, not in terms of events but in terms of beingness or future achievements.

Those who act as psychics and tell us about future events such as earthquakes, storms, fires, epidemics, drought, or the death of prominent people are those whose astral body is highly developed because of the energy imparted to it through the love petals. The astral body is connected to the Chalice through the astral permanent atom and through the petals active in the astral body. Because of the development of the astral body, the psychic can at times tune to the Intuitional Plane and bring out certain information about the future. But because his mental body is not developed, he misinterprets the events that he is receiving through his astral hearing and astral vision.

This is why these "prophets" are mostly misleading, and their words are mistranslated and misapplied. If these psychics review the list of their prophecies with a detached consciousness, they will see how erroneous their prophecies were. It is worse when, because of certain prejudices, these psychics consciously distort their prophecies for material gain.

There are also psychics who have one or two petals developed in their mental body and are clairvoyant and clairaudient in the mental plane. Their prophecies are better in quality than those who were working in the astral plane, but, again, their prophecies are limited due to the thoughtforms crystallized on the fourth level of the mental plane.

Our consciousness does not leave the fourth level of the mental plane until the nine petals of the Lotus are fully unfolded. It is such an unfoldment that allows the consciousness of man to be focused on the higher mental plane.

During the unfolding period of the third tier petals, our consciousness travels from the third to the second and then to the first level of the mental plane and becomes ready to pass into the Intuitional Plane during the destruction of the Temple of Solomon — the Chalice. This progress is based on the intensity of striving of the human soul, his past karma, and the help given by a Great One to lead the person from darkness to light.

We must not forget that all our progress is based on our

Striving

Past karma

Past and present service

Solar Angel

Master

We often forget our Master and His assistance given to us throughout ages as we proceeded on the Path and had certain achievements. Behind most of our accomplishments and achievements exists the One Who silently inspired, encouraged, guided, protected, enlightened, warned, and healed us throughout time. How deep should be our gratitude to the invisible Helpers Who watched over our evolution age after age, especially when we passed through the crisis of the unfolding of our petals.

60 | The Chalice and Motion

When we think about the causal body, we think about it as if it were a stationary body, like a planted flower which in due time grows up and opens its petals. But we forget the most important mystery of it. The Lotus, or the causal body, rotates on its axis.

This rotation is related to the zodiacal signs. Each month it orients itself to one of the signs of the zodiac, and, according to its unfoldment and opened petals, it absorbs energy from the higher sources to nourish the spark in its womb.

When the highest petals start opening, the Lotus contacts the signs of the bigger zodiac, such as the Great Bear, Sirius, and Pleiades. As the Lotus rotates, it has three functions: It *receives energy, assimilates energy,* and *distributes energy* to the centers existing in the physical, emotional, and mental bodies, bringing coordination among them.

Rotation also helps the Lotus to fuse the energies received into one current of energy, charging it with various precious elements.

Not only the Chalice as a whole rotates on its axis, but also the petals rotate on their own axis and revolve around the Jewel in the Lotus.

The atoms forming the multi-colored aura of the Lotus move in a spiral, making the Lotus appear to be perpetually going up and up.

Each movement has its purpose and practical effect on the person. All the movements of the Chalice and its petals are conditioned or orchestrated by the cyclic and rhythmic pulsation of the Jewel in the Lotus — the real human being in embryo.

One must develop the power of visualization to understand the beauty of the Lotus and its movements. The movements of the Lotus eventually will synchronize with the movements of each sign of the zodiac.

When the Lotus is destroyed, its role is transferred to the Spiritual Triad, which again is in constant motion with the rest of the Universe at the Fifth Initiation.

61 | The Three Laws and the Chalice

In one of the esoteric books of the East it is written: "The Monads are seeds of sacrifice, coming to the Cosmic Physical Plane to emancipate and liberate the divinity living in all matter, atoms, and forms."

Sacrifice actually means to bring out and manifest the divinity that is your Core. To be able to manifest this divinity within you, you need to actualize three laws that bring their assistance or punishment to the incarnating Monad.

The first law is the **Law of Economy,** which means to use your time, body, money, life, and all that you have and you are for the purpose of manifesting your divinity.

If you do not use all that you have purposefully or goalfittingly, the Law of Economy turns against you and takes from your hand all that you have.

The cause of the destruction of Atlantis and the devastation of Sodom and Gomorrah was *waste* — waste of time, indulgence; waste of the human seed; waste of money; waste of energy, food, space, and time for the pleasure of the body, for showing off, vanity, ego, or for sex or for the six vipers of fear, anger, hatred, jealousy, revenge, and slander.

The next law is the **Law of Attraction and Repulsion**, which is really the Law of Discrimination: how close to go, how far away to go. If you go too close, you will burn yourself. If you go too far, you lose yourself.

The third law is the **Law of Synthesis**. The Law of Synthesis is actually the Law of Withdrawal into the True Values, trying to touch the All Self through the actualization of your True Self.

— The Law of Economy is for the physical, emotional, and mental man.

— The Law of Attraction and Repulsion is for the human soul.

— The Law of Synthesis is for Initiates.

These laws have to be observed in the individual field, family field, group field, national field, and the field of humanity.

You must have the eye to see what happens to individuals who do not observe these laws. For example, if vanity, ego, showing off, and the six vipers lead you to waste your time, energy, money, and body, in this life and in the next life you will be put into conditions in which you will starve. This is true for individuals, families, groups, nations, and humanity.

On the other hand, stinginess and greed are considered actions of economy, which they are not. Stinginess is an act of burying the treasure given to you, as the money that was kept by the servant of the rich man in the New Testament parable. The right and purposeful use and purposeful circulation of energy is economy.

Greed is considered economy, but again it is the imprisonment of treasures and an act of stealing from others.

These three laws are related to the three fires and to the petals of the Lotus.

Unfolding the knowledge petals eventually brings the latent and vital or pranic fires together and fuses them around the heart center between the shoulder blades.

Unfolding the love petals eventually brings the vital or pranic and latent fire to fusion with the mental fire at the bottom of the skull.

Unfolding the sacrifice petals eventually brings the fusion of all these fires with the fire of Spirit above the top of the head. Thus, fire of matter and fire of Soul and fire of Spirit meet, and man achieves his mastery.

We must remember that it is through expansion of consciousness that all this is accomplished, not by any method of mechanical exercises or rituals.

— The Law of Synthesis is related to Electric Fire.

— The Law of Attraction and Repulsion is related to Solar Fire.

— The Law of Economy is related to Fire by Friction.

These three laws are represented in the Chalice: the Law of Economy in the knowledge petals, the Law of Attraction and Repulsion in the love petals, and the Law of Synthesis in the sacrifice petals.

When abiding by the Law of Economy, you unfold the knowledge petals and you raise the *ida* fire from the base of the spine.[1]

When you unfold the love petals through abiding by the Law of Attraction and Repulsion, you raise the *pingala* fire.

When you unfold the sacrifice petals through abiding by the Law of Sacrifice, you raise the *sushumna* fire.

---

1.   See also "The Kundalini Fire," Ch. 12, in *New Dimensions in Healing*.

62 | Enthusiasm and the Chalice

Enthusiasm creates communication lines within our whole system. It integrates our three lower vehicles. It creates discipline, striving, and unfoldment.

Our vehicles become sensitive through the fire of increasing enthusiasm. Enthusiasm creates integration among the physical, etheric, emotional, and mental bodies, which in the fire of enthusiasm function as one unit.

Enthusiasm creates discipline. The vehicles adjust themselves to the rhythm of the increasing fire of the higher principles and laws.

Enthusiasm quickens the human soul who begins to strive to expand his consciousness. He uses his vehicles to receive more energy and uses them for the Common Good.

It is through the fire of enthusiasm that the petals of the Chalice unfold. As this fire increases within the human soul, it exercises pressure upon the petals of the Chalice, and they unfold their sound, color, and fragrance.

Enthusiasm is the fire of the spirit, the electrical fire coming from the Core of the Monad. Human progress, until the end of the Fourth Initiation, is related to and conditioned by the unfoldment of the petals of the Chalice. Each petal of the Chalice influences all our physical, emotional, and mental natures, affecting our cells, organs, glands, nervous system, blood, centers, and their correspondences in our physical, emotional, and mental planes. Furthermore, the unfoldment of the petals of the Chalice determines the quantity and quality of the emanations of our electromagnetic currents which determine our influence in life and our success and achievements.

Each unfolding petal expands our consciousness and the space in which our consciousness functions.

The unfolding petals determine our communication with higher planes and the spheres of the Higher Worlds.

All this is accomplished by the increasing fire of enthusiasm. It is so important that we cherish the sparks of enthusiasm in our daily labor, in our relationships, in our creativity and service to make them eventually currents of ever-flowing and everlasting energy in our aura, to inspire striving, discipline, and unfoldment in others, and to move the wheel of continuous evolution forward for the good of all living beings.

The fire of enthusiasm increases as it is used in all our labor and relationships. As we increase its fire in our system, the created heat affects the Chalice and causes its petals to unfold with their radiant beauty. This is the flowering of the seed of the Spark, the human soul.

The human soul must accomplish his blooming, thus creating a link between the highest and the lowest, between the unmanifested and the manifested. And when this link and fusion are created, the duty of the human soul is to burn away the mechanism, the Chalice, and establish the continuity of fusion with the Higher Worlds.

The treasures accumulated in the Chalice are used as materials for bridges extending toward the Higher Worlds, and all this is done by the fire of increasing enthusiasm.

The future success and greatness of children can be foreseen through the degree of this enthusiasm. Those who show enthusiasm in their studies, creative works, and service already have unfolding petals.

The fire of enthusiasm not only helps them unfold their petals further, but it also creates the shield around them to protect them from attacks of physical, moral, and mental pollution. The nature of enthusiasm, being fire, does not allow disintegrating factors to penetrate into the threefold vehicles of the child. Thus the child is protected on the way to his destination.

A few charged children or persons can create unfoldment of consciousness in the area where they live. Often their influence extends beyond their group, school, nation, and reaches humanity.

Enthusiasm, like a fire, can jump from country to country and create unfoldment, progress, and fruitful service.

In the future, people will discover the laws and principles of this fire and create one of the most needed sciences, the science of enthusiasm.

People think that the fire of enthusiasm is an abstract concept, but it is not. It is possible to see this fire, its color and flow, its effect on human labor. It is as real as electricity, which is the lowest manifestation of the fire of enthusiasm in form.

When certain scientists unfold their seventh petal, then it will be possible for them to create the science of enthusiasm and use this energy to

— Enlighten people

— Heal people

— Transform people

— Make them real

— Change our culture and civilization

— Guide people to the Purpose of life

63 | Sensitivity and the Chalice

In the esoteric Teaching, sensitivity is the ability to register and record impressions that are not only physical, emotional, and mental but are even higher, such as intuitional, atmic, monadic or global, solar, and galactic. This sensitivity is developed and refined as the petals of the Chalice unfold and expand their colors and radiation.

When the nine petals of the Chalice are in the process of unfolding, they are related to impressions coming from the physical, emotional, and mental planes. When the fourth tier petals begin to develop, the sensitivity of all the petals become multidimensional. For example, knowledge petals not only bring impressions from the three lower planes but also from their correspondences found in individual, planetary, and solar existences because the petals resonate with the Chalices of planetary and solar Beings. The love petals not only bring impressions from the three lower planes but also from planetary and solar astral planes. The sacrifice petals not only bring impressions from the three lower planes but also from planetary and solar mental planes.

Toward the last stages of development of the fourth tier petals, the Chalice as a whole becomes sensitive to the Galactic Heart and prepares the person to be a Master of Wisdom.

M.M. says,

> *The magnet of the spirit, this propellent aggregator of the life energies, is nurtured by the manifestation of the cosmic energy. The accumulations in the Chalice gather around the seed of the spirit, enveloping it in their colors. The very striving seed of the spirit responds to the fiery impulsion. Thus, the magnet of the spirit of an Agni Yogi is the creative sower of the affirmed fires. Verily, the sower of cosmic fires into the consciousness of men is a true co-worker of Cosmos.* [1]

> *The sensing of the quivering of the ground and the sensing of the moving of clouds should be recorded. Subtlety of receptivity is bestowed upon the refined Carrier of the Chalice. The assimilation of subtle fires*

---

1.   *Infinity*, Vol. II, para. 35.

can yield manifestations attainable in higher spheres.[2]

In the future, we are told, the World Teacher will give us the advanced science of impression. The Chalice is related to the impressions coming from the higher mind, intuitional, and still higher spheres.

The nine petals of the Chalice are first one-dimensional. When the fourth tier petals begin to unfold, they play a second and third dimensional role, preparing the man to achieve mastery over the lower worlds. What this means is that the three knowledge, three love, and three sacrifice petals extend not only into the three lower bodies of man but also into the physical, emotional, and mental bodies of the planet and solar system, and the consciousness of man expands to translate impressions reaching him from these lofty spheres.

When the human soul begins to function in the Spiritual Triad, the consciousness of the Initiate begins to expand into the galactic consciousness.

During such an unfoldment, the petals of the Chalice serve as receivers, assimilators, translators, and transmitters.

Later, the higher impressions received by the Spiritual Triad are assimilated, translated, and transmitted by the thousand-petaled Lotus in the head center, each petal having a specialized duty in harmony with the rest of the petals and in harmony with the planetary, solar, and galactic Chalices.

---

2. *Ibid.*, para. 22.

64 | Construction of the Network

The construction of the Chalice is one of the supreme labors of a human being.

The Chalice is the person's home in the Higher Worlds, a place where he learns the science of using energies and forces.

Energies come from the Higher Worlds, and they become forces directed to the three lower worlds.

The building of the Chalice is one labor; to equip it with treasures is another labor; to use it for creative ends and serve the evolution of Life is the third labor.

It is through the Chalice that the human soul consciously comes in contact with the threefold vehicles — physical, emotional, and mental — via the three permanent atoms. The human soul learns the art of using these three vehicles as he unfolds petal after petal, using the energy radiating through the unfolding petals.

The objective of the human soul is to establish a network of communication lines between the Chalice and the personality vehicles. Eventually the human soul controls the vehicles and builds them up in such a way that he can use them for his objectives and goals.

Only through the unfolding Chalice will the human soul have the wisdom and energies to perfect his bodies, organize in them the network of centers and senses to the maximum degree, and use them as perfect communication devices for their corresponding spheres.

The evolution and reconstruction of our bodies still wait for the time when the human soul will truly understand their nature and scientifically work on them to make them reach the highest perfection possible on this planet.

Another labor of the human soul will be to build the bridge between the mental unit and the Mental Permanent Atom existing on the highest level of the mental plane. When this is achieved, the human soul will have continuity of consciousness on the physical, astral, and mental planes simultaneously. This will be a great achievement and will have a great affect on his personal life and surroundings.

The next labor of the human soul will be gradually to build communication lines with the Intuitional and Atmic Permanent Atoms to secure his future move into the Spiritual Triad. In the Spiritual Triad he will clearly understand the Plan of the Hierarchy and cooperate with the Hierarchy for the actualization of the Plan on earth.

After so many millions of years, humanity and its leaders do not yet see the Divine Plan and do not see that humanity is moving toward it.

All pain and suffering experienced by humanity is nothing else but the result of its ignorance and selfish interests. As long as the Plan is not understood, there will be pain and suffering because the energies of the Plan will force humanity to live according to the Plan or else perish.

It is in the Chalice that the first glimpses of the Plan are seen. Cooperation with the Plan is carried out in its full measure in the Spiritual Triad.

In the Spiritual Triad the Cause behind the Plan is seen.

The human soul, through the Chalice, not only builds the network of communication with the Hierarchy and Shamballa but also with the Chalices of planetary, solar, and galactic Beings. The Chalice is a workshop in which the human soul learns how to solve his individual problems in the three worlds, then learns how to be helpful to others in solving their own problems.

Problems exist because of ignorance and because of reaction to evolutionary forces. Of course, tremendous lessons are learned because of our ignorance, reaction, pain, and suffering. But the time will come when the human soul will scientifically cooperate with the evolutionary forces and not create friction. This will be the turning point in his life from pain and suffering to real happiness and permanent joy.

As the human soul succeeds in building better vehicles, he will also learn how to read the "history" of his journey in his own permanent atoms. The permanent atoms are the permanent recorders. Without being able to read these records, the soul will not succeed in understanding many events or solving many problems.

The permanent atoms, like diskettes, are connected to the "Big Computer" of some of the Karmic Lords, Who then have immediate access to your recordings. This is how They prepare your karma throughout the history of your journey.

65 | The Destruction of the Chalice

In the process of growth, a time comes when the human soul is ready for birth and the Chalice is no longer needed. The human soul is now an embodiment of Light, Love, and Sacrifice.

In *A Treatise on Cosmic Fire*, fascinating details are given about how the Chalice is destroyed.

The central fire in the Chalice is the fire of love and the embodiment of love. This nucleus of love extends its force to the physical permanent atom, which in its turn transmits this force — in the form of five rays — to the astral permanent atom. As the relationship of these two atoms increases, their light merges and they act as a fiery unit. This happens as the human soul proceeds on the Path of initiation.

Then this fiery unit attracts the mental unit and eventually unites, merges with it, and forms one unit.

Then the central fire within the Lotus draws these three fires and synthesizes them in its fire.

The intensity of these fires reaches such a high degree that it burns the petals of the Chalice and passes to the higher planes of existence.

This process, of course, takes lives until a man enters the Fourth Initiation and transfers his consciousness into the Intuitional Plane.

This process shows how the physical permanent atom, through its radioactivity, purifies and brings into perfection the etheric body and all its network of etheric centers. After this accomplishment, the physical permanent atom energizes the astral permanent atom with five streams of energy. These energies dissolve the accumulations of glamors in the astral body and create fusion between the two atoms.

It is this fusion that fuses the etheric and astral bodies, and the human consciousness begins to function also upon the astral plane. Furthermore, these two atoms involve the mental unit and eventually fuse with it. It is this fusion that slowly brings to the surface all that is impressed within the fifth, sixth, and seventh layers of the mind — the subconscious mind.

As the fusion and synthesis approach the central fire of the Lotus and the three permanent atoms, the surfacing elements of the subconscious mind begin to burn the glamors of the astral body and the illusions of the lower mind, and the person reaches the stage of Transfiguration.

When the whole personality is purified, the human soul enters the Fourth Initiation. The essential fire within destroys the Chalice and distributes the treasure in the

Chalice into the consciousness of humanity. After withdrawing from the Chalice, the human soul enters the Spiritual Triad.

Every time a human soul passes into the Spiritual Triad, he leaves behind many treasures for humanity. All his creative expressions, his heroic service and example, and his unseen treasures are given to the wings of Space, ready to be accepted by those who have developed their Chalice.

Those who penetrate into the Spiritual Triad still can live upon the physical plane, if they choose, as the Masters of Wisdom.

66 | Various Chalices

The Tibetan Master, says that there are various kinds of Chalices or Lotuses.

First, there are young Lotuses which have at least one petal open. The petals open according to the evolution of the human soul. The more advanced you are, the more unfolding petals you have.

The Lotuses of "third class creators" are those whose first knowledge petal is open. These are the active people — laborers, agriculturists, peasants — who are eager to improve their life through hard labor.

Then, there are "second class creators" who are a little more evolved than the previous ones. The Tibetan Master says that these human souls are originally from Venus or Jupiter. They have two petals unfolded, and thus they have love in their activities.

Next, we have "primary lotuses" which are under the line of the Lord of the Fifth Ray and which demonstrate mental activity. The Tibetan Master says that "they were quiescent during the Atlantean root-race but have come in during the fourth and fifth subraces of this root-race."[1]

They have the first and third of the knowledge petals open, but the middle one, which is related to love, still needs to open.

"They may be seen in the purely intellectual selfish scientific type. They are responsible for much of the advanced application of mechanical science to the needs of men, and for the introduction of certain types of machinery; they work largely in connection with the energy of the mineral kingdom. . . .Their work for the race has at present a deleterious effect, but when the second petal is opened, the wonders then to be achieved by them in loving service along their own particular line will be one of the factors which will regenerate the fourth kingdom."[2]

Then, we have Lotuses called "lotuses of passion and desire." They are on the line of love, and they are the "well-to-do, kindly people of the world." These people have two petals unfolded, and they are developing the third petal.

Of course, there are many other kinds of Lotuses. Each one is different from the others because of its origins and because of the number of its unfolded petals.

Another reason for the difference is due to the kind of Monad it carries. According to the Teaching, we have

---

1.   Alice A. Bailey, *A Treatise on Cosmic Fire*, p. 841.
2.   *Ibid.*, p. 842.

Monads of will, Monads of love, and Monads of active intelligence. These three factors also condition the variations between the Lotuses.

The difference between people and the difference between nations is the difference of the degree of the unfoldment of the petals. The more unfolded petals we have, the more that right human relations will rule the earth and the more peace and the more cooperation we will have.

67 | The Petals and the Three Halls

The three halls are three states of consciousness through which a person passes until he leaves these three halls behind. Symbolically they are called

The Hall of Ignorance

The Hall of Learning

The Hall of Wisdom

The first one is the world of the physical plane in which we wander for millions of years until we enter the astral plane, which is the Hall of Learning.

The Hall of Wisdom starts from the lower mental plane, and level by level enters the higher mind, and then the Spiritual Triad.

The Hall of Ignorance is related to the first tier of the Lotus, the knowledge petals. The Hall of Learning is related to the love petals. The Hall of Wisdom is related to the petals of sacrifice.

In the Hall of Ignorance we are interested in matter, ego, separatism, greed. In the Hall of Learning the Solar Angel tries to awaken the human soul and help him cultivate virtues. Virtues slowly create equilibrium between the form and the spiritual side of man. In the Hall of Wisdom the human soul develops mastery over the threefold personality and gradually manifests his inner and divine potentials.

In the Hall of Ignorance the intelligence principle is active in the person, but he does not have love. In the Hall of Learning the person becomes aware of the existence of pure love. Love creates relations, affiliations, and groupings. In the Hall of Wisdom the person begins to relate himself to will energy and uses it for sacrificial labor.

In the Hall of Wisdom the higher Teaching is related to the Teaching that the coming Sixth and Seventh Races will practice in their daily life. The principles and standards of the future two Races are given in the Hall of Wisdom in the higher levels of the mental plane.

These three halls are not three classes, but they are like graded schools. It is possible that each hall has seven grades. Ignorance is darkness in the first grade. In the third grade the personality is the main interest. Then comes self-interest, then comes sex. The laws of the physical world are taught.

In the Hall of Learning, the gradation is similar. The students are taught

- Virtues

- Self-control

- Right human relations

- Wisdom-religion

- Symbolism

In the Hall of Wisdom:

- They meet their Master

- They are given specialized Teaching in

  — sacrificial service

  — leadership

  — divine laws

  — synthesis, unity

  — building the higher Antahkarana

There they are divided into three Rays, and each group receives proper wisdom in his own field of labor. To be able to function in the Hall of Wisdom one must be cleaned of ego, vanity, greed, separatism, and fanaticism, have an expanding consciousness, and have an unfolding Chalice.

In the Hall of Learning one develops his astral body and his astral centers and senses, and he makes them a healthy, pure, and organized mechanism.

In these subjective halls, where people visit for subjective education, one major instruction is given: how to remember the Teaching in waking consciousness. This is so important because if a man develops his *memory* of the classes, he can turn into a source of the most creative and modern ideas and vision and gain leadership in these fields where he is active.

The Tibetan Master says, "Those who are to teach the world more about the Masters and who are being trained to be focal points of contact are put through a very drastic disciplining. They are tested in every possible way and taught much through bitter experience. They are taught to attach no importance to recognition. They are trained not to judge from the appearance but from the inner vision. Capacity to recognize the Master's purpose and the ability to love are counted of paramount importance. Aspirants who seek to be chosen for work as disciples must lose all desire for the things of self and must be willing at any cost to pay the price of knowledge."[1]

The Tibetan Master gives some very important information in *A Treatise on Cosmic Fire* about these three halls. He says,

> "*Within the Hall of Ignorance* kama-manas rules. The man, weighed down by much misplaced desire, seeks for the object of his heart's attention within the murky halls of

1.   Alice A. Bailey, *A Treatise on White Magic*, pp. 350-351.

densest maya. He finds it there but dies ere garnering all the longed-for fruit. The serpent stings him, and the joy desired recedes from out his grasp. All seeking thus the selfish fruits of karma must each despise each other; hence strife and greed, ill-will and hatred, death and retribution, karmic invocation and the thunderbolt of vengeance characterise this Hall.

"*Within the Hall of Learning* intellect rules and seeks to guide. Desire of a higher kind, the fruit of manas and its use, supplants the lower kamic urge. Man weighs and balances, and in the twilight Halls of Intellection seeks for the fruit of knowledge. He finds it but to realize that knowledge is not all; he dies upon the open field of knowledge, hearing a cry beat on his dying ears: 'Know that the knower greater is than knowledge; the One who seeks is greater than the sought.'

"*Within the Hall of Wisdom* the Spirit rules; the One within the lesser ones assumes supreme control. Death is not known within these halls, for its two great gates are passed. Discord and strife both disappear and only harmony is seen. The knowers see themselves as One; they recognize the field wherein knowledge grows as Brahmic dissonance and differentiation. Knowledge they know as method, an instrument of purpose utilized by all and just a germ of eventual recognition. Within this hall union of each with each,

blending of one and all, and unity of action, goal
and skill marks every high endeavor."[2]

"Classes are held by initiates of the first and
second degrees, for accepted disciples and those
on probation, between the hours of ten and five
every night in all parts of the world, so that the
continuity of the teaching is complete."[3]

Those disciples who have developed continuity of
consciousness need not necessarily sleep during these
hours to receive instruction. They, in their waking consciousness, receive the impressions from the classes and
record them in their mind. It is a matter of tuning in to
these currents of energies which emanate especially from
the Hall of Learning and the Hall of Wisdom.

But, of course, during sleep most people easily assimilate the Teaching of the classes, and they feel that they
must not waste their time in front of television or at parties
while the classes are going on.

Neophytes are advised not to use alcohol nor fill their
consciousness with programs of violence before they
sleep.

---

2. Alice A. Bailey, *A Treatise on Cosmic Fire*, pp. 849-850.
3. Alice A. Bailey, *Initiation, Human and Solar* (New York: Lucis
   Publishing Co., 1977), p. 64.

68 | Initiations and the Petals of the Lotus

We are told in general that at the first, the second, and Third Initiations, one of the three tiers of petals opens up, and during the Fourth Initiation the petals ten, eleven, and twelve unfold and release the Jewel in the Lotus, which in intense heat burns up the Chalice.

The Tibetan Master says that during the first initiation, petal numbers one, two, and three of knowledge unfold. In the second initiation the love petals — four, five, and six — unfold, and in the Third Initiation the sacrifice petals — seven, eight, and nine — unfold. This is called the Transfiguration Initiation, which is completed by the fusion of the three energies of light, love, and power.

At the Fourth Initiation the petals of the fourth tier — ten, eleven, and twelve — unfold and the human soul becomes ready to enter into the Fifth Initiation after the destruction of the Chalice.

In the process of unfoldment of the petals, the Rays of the Monad play a great role.

There are three major types of Monads:

Monads of power

Monads of love

Monads of activity

The Monads of love, we are told, are easily awakened because the majority of human beings have Second Ray souls. Monads of activity are "numerous and influential," says the Tibetan Master, and for them it is easy to open the first petal of each three tiers.

As far as the sacrifice petals are concerned, they are not easily opened, and generally the Initiate must wait until he enters into the Third Initiation.

The petals relate also to the three halls. For example, through the Hall of Ignorance, in pain and suffering, the three knowledge petals open.

The petals of love are organized and unfolded in the Hall of Learning.

The petals of sacrifice are organized and unfolded in the Hall of Wisdom.

With the three tiers of petals unfolding, one of the three groups of Solar Angels who are related to the Chalice are affected.

It is very interesting to see how the Chalice is related not only to initiation but also to each etheric center, to their petals, and to the three halls.

Through meditation and service, the unfoldment and coordination of the Chalice with other networks of light of the human beings is accomplished.

All these unfoldments are to lead us to Arhathood, to the Fourth Initiation in which all twelve petals are unfolded with color and beauty.

For the first initiation, the first petal of the first tier begins to open. This leads the initiate toward searching in physical, emotional, and mental causes of events. With the second petal, this urge deepens but relates more to the emotions. With the third petal, the search is directed more to the mental plane. One cannot get real answers to his questions yet because his questions are not yet formalized.

For the second initiation, he enters into the Hall of Learning. He learns from his physical experiences, emotional and mental experiences, having, in the meantime, flashes of light of the Intuition. The mind he uses is mostly the higher mind, and he deals with the events of life.

The first petal of love brings him closer to a group outlook. The second petal of love brings his outlook closer to a racial outlook. The third petal of love brings him closer to a planetary outlook.

For the Third Initiation, the petals of sacrifice begin to unfold and lead the Initiate to the Hall of Wisdom. The first petal of sacrifice urges the Initiate to serve in physical plane life. The second petal of sacrifice urges the Initiate to serve in the astral plane. The third petal of sacrifice urges the Initiate to serve on the mental plane with Intuition illuminating all his activities.

In the first initiation, the person rotates around his own axis. In the second initiation, he is a planet revolving around the Sun — a Teacher, an ideal, etc. In the Third Initiation, he has cyclic, forward moving, spiral motion around a greater center.

In the Hall of Ignorance, he eventually controls the physical body when his third petal opens. Here inertia is conquered. In the Hall of Learning, he eventually controls the astral plane when the sixth petal opens. Here glamor is conquered. In the Hall of Wisdom, he eventually controls the mental plane when the ninth petal opens. Here illusion is conquered.

In the Fourth Initiation, the Dweller on the Threshold is conquered, and the astral plane is dissipated.

In religious literature, the Hall of Ignorance is called the outer court. The Hall of Learning is called the Sanctuary. The Hall of Wisdom is called the Holy of Holies, where only an Initiate of Transfiguration can enter as a contact point between man and the Supermundane Worlds.

69 | The Chalice of Ashramic Groups

The Chalice of ashramic groups develops the same way as an individual's Lotus. What makes a group ashramic is that the leader, or one of the guides in the group, has relations with Great Ones through the Intuitional Plane and is an accepted disciple or an Initiate of the Third Degree.

As the Chalice of a group leader builds up and unfolds, his radiance and service increase in the world. Simultaneously, when the group is ready, certain devas provide their essence to start a group Chalice and one of them acts as the Solar Angel of the group.

As the group increases in pure esoteric knowledge, it becomes all giving, all forgiving, all inclusive, all striving, all synthesizing, has an all sacrificial will, and the

Chalice grows and expands. The Chalice then becomes a bank for all spiritual treasures of the group activities, group love and cooperation, group sacrifice and beauty.

When the group Chalice increases its treasures, people in the group can share these treasures in times of emergency and need through the petals of their individual Chalices.

Treason against the group can have dire consequences in the lives of those who commit it. Such a treason acts not only against each member of the ashramic group, but also against the group Solar Angel Who feels a setback in His plans for the group.

The Evolutionary Law exists to create individual, group, national, and global Chalices. Failure in building these Chalices leads to calamities, pain, and suffering. Those who cause such setbacks are traitors known by many names such as Judas and Devadattas. They not only harm the group Chalice, but they also destroy the petals of their own Chalice and for a long time experience depression, loneliness, confusion, and the resulting physical, emotional, and mental ailments.

Sometimes they suffer for many lives before they once again enter the "road of builders." Those who are Masons will understand how the building of the Temple proceeds and why every Mason is, in the meantime, a builder and also a stone.

The formation of the scheme and the solar system follow the same principles, and the Builders attract the same or similar traitors who are eventually cast away and burned by the electrical fire of the Supreme.

Any group in the world in any field of human endeavor can be admitted into the ranks of ashramic groups. The key is group cooperation in the spirit of Beauty,

Goodness, Righteousness, Joy, Freedom, Striving, and Sacrificial service. It is those elements that conceive the Chalice and attract Great Builders. When the Chalice reaches a certain perfection, the Hierarchy recognizes the group and accepts it as an ashramic group.

An ashramic group is one that is devoted in all its activities to building

- a healthy world

- a peaceful, loving, united humanity

- an enlightened, creative humanity

- a humanity striving toward perfection

An ashramic group lives to serve the Kingdom of God — the Plan.

If the nine petals are all open, an ashramic group is in balance. Balance is a great principle; without it progress, creativity, health, and happiness are impossible. The real nature of balance is to have a right proportion of knowledge, love, and sacrifice within each of our actions, emotions, words, and thoughts. Light must be balanced by love; light and love must be balanced by sacrificial energy.

This Trinity is expressed in the triangle of Light, Love, and Power. When the balance is broken, a man or a group falls into error and builds a powerful karma. Excess light, excess love, and excess power, uncontrolled and out of balance with each other, can devastate individuals, groups, and nations. That is why, when we read about certain disturbances, wars, revolutions, suffering, and turmoil in nations, we know that there is a lack of balance in them.

The closer we get to a state of balance, the more happiness shines in the life of the planet.

Great Teachers in all fields come to restore the balance and lead us to Synthesis.

Education at the present is not in balance. There is too much knowledge and very little love and little striving toward perfection. Education can create a balanced society if all that it imparts is based on truth and fact, charged and inspired by love, if its intention is to use that knowledge for all men everywhere, and if it is galvanized by the power to live for all that exists. It may take another two thousand years for education to realize this, but if those who know take action, they may prevent possible calamities in the future as a result of unbalanced education.

Thus, if the petals of humanity do not unfold and grow harmoniously, the Greater Chalices in Space will exercise tremendous pressure on them at the appointed time and cause disintegration in them. This is what happened to the Lemurian and Atlantean Races. Their racial Chalices were dissolved for millions of ages, losing all the treasures collected in them. Those who had their individual Chalices built kept some of the treasure in the Chalice, and that is the origin of the Ageless Wisdom.

Balance is achieved by increasing your knowledge, love, and sacrificial life in equal proportion. Unless you are balanced, you do not have a chance to survive. Ask a surfer who surfs on twenty foot waves what is the secret that keeps him on the waves. He will say, "Balance." Balance is the key to survival. A bird flies and an airplane glides in the air because of balance.

Imbalance is the origin of pain, suffering, and death. Fanaticism and separatism are the result of imbalance. When you receive letters, when you read books, or when you meet people, try to see if there is balance in them. If there is no balance in them, be extremely cautious.

Lack of balance often means mental, emotional, and physical disturbances which may cause unnecessary troubles in your life.

A girl came to work in our office. She said, "I love my boyfriend, but I hate my father and mother."

I said, "You have no balance."

I watched her life as she fell into one failure after another and did not learn how to balance herself.

An imbalanced life creates an imbalanced beingness.

The more your Lotus blooms, the less karma you have. All your karma is related to the Lotus. That is why it is called also the "causal body."

The recordings of the permanent atoms and the treasure of the Chalice decide the form and conditions of your lives to come.

70 | The Chalice and Initiations

There are very close communications between the Chalice and Planetary and Solar Logoi and between the Chalice and the human physical brain. It is this relationship that enables man to speed the evolution of his bodies and unfold psychic potentials sleeping within his soul. Such communications of the Chalice with higher and lower worlds deepens during the moments that the person takes initiation.

For example, in the second initiation, the first and second tiers of the petals are usually unfolded. In the Third Initiation, nine petals are unfolded. In the Fourth Initiation, twelve petals are unfolded.

During the initiation the Initiate stands in the center of a triangle which is formed by a Deva and two Masters.

At the right moment a stream of energy from the Solar Logos is released and, passing through the Planetary Logos, reaches the Monad of the Initiate. The Three Great Ones act as protective agents and as equilibrating agents for the Initiate.

The fire is released from the Higher Sources, three times circulating through these Three Great Ones and through the Rod of the Initiator. The fiery energy in the Monad of the Initiate is brought down to his three tiers of petals of the Lotus, and then from these three tiers of petals to one petal, using it as a channel to reach one of the permanent atoms, then to the three higher etheric centers, and ending in the brain of the Initiate.

The petals and centers are chosen according to the Ray and evolution of man. Thus, during the Third Initiation the Lotus of the Initiate turns into a communication network between higher and lower worlds.

The need for purity is emphasized in the Teaching — mental, astral, and physical purity. The reason is that the Initiate cannot stand in the center of the Triangle of Fire and receive the Divine Fire if his bodies are not highly purified. This is why from the beginning the Teaching emphasizes purity in thinking, emotions, expressions, and deeds.

The more we purify the bodies, the closer we get to the day of an initiation. When a person consciously operates in the Lotus, he can use the higher energies to bring great changes in himself and in the world as a whole. He not only becomes a source of higher creativity, but also his energy leads, destroys obstacles, illuminates, and reveals the eternal Purpose of existence.

As the Initiate serves to illuminate people and the world, he moves to the Intuitional Plane and stands in the center of the Spiritual Triad. It is through this move that man liberates himself from the limitations of time and space.

An Initiate is a rare beauty. In the subtle world he appears as a Rainbow or as a radioactive Diamond.

Initiations are a result of the unfolding of the petals of the Chalice. You cannot take initiations unless your petals are unfolding in healthy and natural ways due to your meditation, sacrificial service, and striving.

In the first initiation you must have four petals unfolded. In the second initiation you must have the fifth, the sixth, the seventh, and the eighth petal unfolded.[1] In the Third Initiation your nine petals must be unfolded. It takes a long time to see the real colors of the petals — translucent, and extremely sensitive to higher influences.

In the Fourth Initiation, the petals of the fourth tier begin to unfold with their pure, lemon yellow, translucent colors. As they unfold, you can see a blue light radiating out from the Core. At that time, a ray of light comes from a High Being, increasing the fire of the flame to such a degree that suddenly it burns all the petals and the Chalice disappears in a blaze of many colors and light. Man is now an Arhat, a Fourth Degree Initiate having the Central Fire.

An Arhat is one who lays down His life for the welfare of humanity. Whatever He is, whatever He has, and whatever He knows is offered to humanity to help it so that one day humanity can become a global Arhat.

---

1. In the first initiation three petals open plus the fourth starts to open to lead the initiate into the second initiation. Similarly, in the second initiation the seventh petal begins to open to a considerable degree to form a bridge for the initiate to enter the Third Initiation.

The human soul now enters the Intuitional Plane through the Mental Permanent Atom, and his awareness slowly focuses itself in the Intuitional Plane. The treasure of the Chalice is now absorbed by the human soul. He is now the Treasury, a result of his own merit and of long ages of striving, service, and sacrifice.

When four petals of the Chalice are unfolded, the human soul achieves control of the physical body. When eight petals are unfolded, he achieves control of the astral body. When the nine petals are unfolded, he achieves control of the mental body, the physical body, and the astral body. Unfoldment of nine petals leads to Transfiguration as the bodies are able to receive the maximum light and fire from the petals of the bud, and all the three bodies radiate light. In Buddhist Teachings, such an achievement is called Enlightenment.

We are told that Buddha achieved Enlightenment under the Bodhi tree after deep contemplation. Jesus achieved Transfiguration on the top of a hill. It was after achieving Transfiguration that both of Them dedicated Themselves to help enlighten humanity.

We learn from *A Treatise on Cosmic Fire* that the Lotus has in itself the threefold power of divinity. The knowledge petals are charges of intelligent energy, which is the source of substance. The love petals are charges of consciousness, related to the psychic nature of man and the Universe, and the sacrifice petals are the charges of electrical fire or energy.[2]

Through the unfoldment of the knowledge petals of the three tiers, man gains power over his threefold

---

2. Alice A. Bailey, *A Treatise on Cosmic Fire*, p. 545.

vehicles. By unfolding the love petals, man gains power over his psychic faculties. By unfolding the three sacrifice petals, he obtains the power of creation or destruction. This power is called the power of lightning. It is the combination of these three energies that in the future will be used by Initiates to communicate, to activate machinery, to control all elementals, and to pass beyond time and space.

These three powers will act through the three eyes of the Initiates with great potency. Behind the eyes of the Inititates exists the power station of the Lotus or the Spiritual Triad.

The unfoldment of the petals is the process of releasing the Cosmic nucleus hidden at the center — the human soul, the Divine Spark, the powers of which are unlimited once the man understands his oneness with all that exists.

The whole Lotus in the higher mind is a vortex of energy and a transmitter of energy. This energy is called psychic energy. It is this energy, controlled by the heart, that brings salvation to humanity. All Great Ones were and are the source and directors of this energy which acts intelligently, with wisdom and power.

Glossary

Adepts: A name given to Masters of Wisdom. Individuals who have mastered the physical, emotional, mental, and Intuitional bodies.

Ageless Wisdom: The sum total of the Teachings given by great Spiritual Teachers throughout time. Also referred to as the Ancient Wisdom, the Teaching, the Ancient Teaching.

Antahkarana: The path, or bridge, between the higher and lower mind, serving as a medium of communication between the two. It is built by the aspirant himself. It is threefold: the consciousness thread, anchored in the brain; the life thread, anchored in the heart; and the creative thread anchored in the throat. More commonly called the Rainbow Bridge or Golden Bridge.

Archetype: The original model from which all things of the same type are copied. The regenerative source of that type.

Arhats: Ancient term designating Fourth Degree Initiates.

Ashram: Sanskrit word. Refers to the gathering of disciples and aspirants which the Master collects for instruction. There are seven major Ashrams, each corresponding to one of the Rays, each forming groups or foci of energy.

Atlantis: (Atlantean Epoch) The continent that was submerged in the Atlantic ocean, according to the occult teaching and Plato. Atlantis was the home of the Fourth Root Race, whom we now call the Atlanteans.

Atmic Plane: The plane of consciousness known as Nirvana, the Third Cosmic Etheric Plane. See Planes.

Causal body: The Chalice in man. See also Lotus.

Centers: Any energy vortex found in a human, planetary, or solar body. Also known as Chakras. Man has seven major centers known as: Base of spine, Sacral, Spleen, Solar Plexus, Heart, Throat, Head.

Central Spiritual Sun: The Core of the Solar System. The Sun is triple: the visible Sun, the Heart of the Sun, and the Central Spiritual Sun.

Deva: Refers to beings following a different line of evolution than the human family.

Disciple: A person who tries to discipline and master his threefold personality, and manifests efficiency in the field where he works and serves.

Divine Plane: The First Cosmic Etheric Plane. See Planes.

Electric Fire: First of three fires of the Universe: Electric Fire, Solar Fire, and Fire by Friction. Energy coming from the Central Spiritual Sun.

Fiery World: Refers to the Mental Plane or above. See Higher Worlds.

Fire by Friction: Third of three fires of the Universe: Electric Fire, Solar Fire, and Fire by Friction. Energy coming from the visible Sun.

Fires, three: See Kundalini.

Fourth Initiation: The Crucifixion Initiation during which the Solar Angel leaves and the Chalice is destroyed by the fully awakened Jewel or Core.

Glamors: Astral forms with a life of their own in the emotional body. When a person desires something intensely, the astral form of that desire is called a glamor. These forms float in a person's aura and connect with certain astral and etheric centers, exercising great power over a person's actions, emotions, thoughts, and relationships. For example, such a person does not like to hear anything against his desires.

Golden Bridge: See Antahkarana.

Head Center: The center which is the synthesis of all seven centers. See Centers.

Heart Center: See Centers.

Hierarchy: The spiritual Hierarchy, whose members have triumphed over matter and have complete control of the personality, or the lower self. Its members are known as Masters of Wisdom Who are custodians of the Plan for humanity and all kingdoms evolving within the sphere of Earth. It is the Hierarchy that translates the Purpose of the Planetary Logos into a Plan for all kingdoms of the planet.

Higher Worlds: Those planes of existence that are of a finer vibration of matter than the physical plane. Generally refers to the higher mental plane and above.

Ida: See Kundalini.

Illusion: Formed when a person has mental contact with inspirations, ideas, visions, revelations, but, due to the inadequately prepared mind, self-centeredness, selfishness, and crystalized thinking, he is unable to translate the incoming energies in their correct form. The resulting illusion is a mistranslation of something factual. Illusions thus contain distorted facts.

Initiate: A person who has taken an initiation.

Initiation: The result of the steady progress of a person toward his life's goals, achieved through service and sacrifice, and manifested as an expansion of his consciousness. It represents a point of achievement marked by a level of enlightenment and awareness. There are a total of nine initiations that the developing human soul must experience in order to reach the Cosmic Heart.

Jewel, The: The Core of the human being; the Monad.

Kama-rupa: The astral body. Kama-manas — lower mind mixed with desire body.

Karma, Law of: The Law of Cause and Effect or attraction and repulsion. "As you sow, so shall you reap."

Krishna: The Teacher or Inner Guide of the hero Arjuna in the story called the Bhagavad Gita. The story symbolizes the unfolding human soul at the transition stage toward Self-awareness.

Kundalini: Three-fold fire in the Base of Spine center, known as the Ida, Pingala, Sushumna fires.

Lemurian civilization: A modern term first used by some naturalists and now adopted by Theosophists to indicate the civilization of the continent Lemuria, which preceded Atlantis. The civilization of the Third Root Race.

Linga-sharira: The etheric body, the cement of the three bodies.

Logos, Planetary: The Soul of the planet. The planet is His dense physical body to provide nourishment for all living forms.

Logos, Solar: The Core of the whole Solar System and all that exists in the Solar System. His purpose is to integrate, correlate and synchronize all Centers using His Light, Love, Power — like an electrical energy — to circulate within each atom through all Centers, thus revealing the Purpose for existence and challenging all forms to strive toward the highest form of cooperation.

Lord Agni: Literally, the Lord of Fire; the Lord of the Cosmic Mental Plane.

Lotus: Also known as the Chalice. Found in the second and third levels of the mental plane (from the top). Formed by twelve different petals of energy: three knowledge petals, three love petals, three sacrifice petals. The three innermost petals of the bud remain folded for ages. They are the dynamic sources of these outer petals. The Lotus contains the essence of all of a person's achievements, true knowledge, and service. It is the dwelling place of the Solar Angel.

Manasic: Mental Substance.

Manvantaras: Periods of activity, or the "days" of the Eternal One.

Masters: Individuals Who had the privilege to master Their physical, emotional, mental, and Intuitional bodies.

Masters of Wisdom: See Hierarchy.

Mental Permanent Atom: See Permanent Atoms.

Mental Unit: A mental mechanism in the fourth level of the mental plane which is formed of four kinds of forces and relates man to the sources of these four forces through its four spirillae.

Monad: See Self.

Neophyte: An aspirant on the path of discipleship.

Obsession: Unconscious state of being under the control of one or more ideas, thoughts, urges, drives, etc.

Permanent Atoms: Each body of a human being has one permanent atom which is the archetype for the construction and constitution of that vehicle in each incarnation.

Pingala: See Kundalini.

Plan, The: The formulation of the Purpose of the Planetary Logos into a workable program — a Plan — by the Planetary Hierarchy for all kingdoms of nature.

Planes: There are seven planes through which a human being travels and which make up human consciousness. From the lowest level upward, they are called: Physical, Emotional or Astral, Mental, Intuitional or Buddhic, Atmic, Monadic, and Divine. The lowest level plane is number seven, and the highest level is number one. Each plane is divided into seven levels.

Possession: Unconscious state of being under the control of one or more disembodied entities.

Psychic energy: The energy of the Central Fire.

Purpose: That which the Solar Logos is intended to achieve at the end of the evolution of the solar system. The Plan is the formulation of this Purpose for our planet only.

Ring-pass-not: Limit of consciousness; veil between present level of being and a higher level requiring a major expansion to penetrate.

Samadhi: Contemplation; a state in which the consciousness is awake on the Intuitional Plane.

Scheme: A vehicle of manifestation of a Planetary Logos composed of seven chains, each composed of seven globes.

Self: The capital "S" Self is another term used to refer to the Core of the human being. The True Self is the developing, unfolding human soul who is trying to liberate himself, go back to his Father, and become his True Self.

Seven Rays: These are the seven primary Rays through which everything exists. They are pure energy, vibrating to a specific frequency and condensing from plane to plane, from manifestation to manifestation. The three primary Rays, or Rays of Aspect, are: The First Ray of Power, Will, and Purpose; The Second Ray of Love-Wisdom; The Third Ray of Active, Creative Intelligence. There are four Rays of Attribute: The Fourth Ray of Harmony Through Conflict; The Fifth Ray of Concrete Science or Knowledge; The Sixth Ray of Idealism or Devotion; The Seventh Ray of Synthesis or Ceremonial Order. These Rays indicate qualities that pertain to the seven fields of human endeavor or expression.

Shamballa: Known as the White Island, it exists in etheric matter and is located in the Gobi Desert. Shamballa is the dwelling place of the Lord of the World, Sanat Kumara, and is the place where "the Will of God is known."

Solar Angels: Very advanced beings Who sacrifice Their life, descending from Higher Worlds to help the evolution of humanity and guide its steps toward initiation. This happened on our planet at the middle of the Lemurian period.

Solar Fire: The Second of three fires of the Universe: Electric Fire, Solar Fire, and Fire by Friction. Energy coming from the Heart of the Sun.

Spiritual Triad: The field of awareness of the human soul. This field comes into existence when the magnetic fields of the

Mental Permanent Atom, the Buddhic Permanent Atom, and the Atmic Permanent Atom fuse and blend.

Subtle World: Refers to the Astral or Emotional Plane.

Subtle Worlds: Refers to all the planes of existence beyond the physical.

Supermundane World: The Higher Worlds.

Sushumna: See Kundalini.

Sutratma: Also known as *The Life Thread*. It is anchored in the heart and acts as the bridge between the spirit and the heart, or the blood stream. It is also called the Life Cord.

Teaching, The: See Ageless Wisdom.

The Tower: The center of the Planetary Council or "where the Will of God is known" or Shamballa.

Thousand-petaled Lotus: The head center, which takes the place of the Chalice after the Fourth Initiation.

Bibliographic References

Agni Yoga Society. New York: Agni Yoga Society.
Brotherhood, 1962.
Infinity, Vol. II, 1957.

Bailey, Alice A. New York: Lucis Publishing Co.
The Beacon Magazine, Sept. / Oct. 1989.
Initiation, Human and Solar, 1977.
Letters on Occult Meditation, 1974.
The Rays and the Initiations, 1976.
A Treatise on Cosmic Fire, 1977.
A Treatise on White Magic, 1972.

Blavatsky, H.P. London: Theosophical Publishing Society.
The Secret Doctrine, 3 vols., 1893.

Blavatsky, H.P. Pasadena, CA: Theosophical University Press.
The Secret Doctrine, 2 vols., 1988.

Blavatsky, H.P. Wheaton, IL: Theosophical Publishing House.
Collected Writings, Vol. XII, 1980.

Lamsa, George M., trans. Nashville, TN: Holman Bible Publishers.
New Testament, 1968.

Saraydarian, Torkom. Sedona, AZ: Aquarian Educational Group.

Cosmos In Man, 1983.

Earthquakes and Disasters — What the Ageless Wisdom Tells Us, 1991.

The Flame of Beauty, Culture, Love, Joy, 1980.

Joy and Healing, 1989.

The Psyche and Psychism, 2 vols., 1981.

The Science of Becoming Oneself, 1976.

The Science of Meditation, 1981.

Sex, Family, and the Woman in Society, 1987.

The Solar Angel, 1990.

Woman, Torch of the Future, 1980.

Saraydarian, Torkom. West Hills, CA: T.S.G. Publishing Foundation, Inc.

The Ageless Wisdom, 1990.

A Commentary on Psychic Energy, 1989.

Cosmic Shocks, 1989.

The Flame of the Heart, 1991.

New Dimensions in Healing, 1992.

Other Worlds, 1991.

The Psychology of Cooperation and Group Consciousness, 1989.

The Purpose of Life, 1991.

The Sense of Responsibility in Society, 1989.

The Seven Rays Interpreted (Video), 1992.

The Year 2000 & After, 1991.

Index

A

Absent-mindedness, 138, 195
Action, wrong
  results of, 340
Actualization, path of, 140,
  207
Adepts, 223, 326-328
Advertisements, 48, 74, 83,
  105-106
Affirmation, 137-140
Age
  and release of subc. mind, 93
Ageless Wisdom, 13-14, 36,
  55, 70, 125, 173, 193, 213,
  240, 267, 281, 297, 310
  objective of, 116
  origin of, 392
Agni Yoga
  See M.M.
Agreements
  and effect of subc. mind, 26
Akasha, 194, 197
Alcohol, 17
  and sleep, 384
  See also Habits
Analysis
  defined, 23
Ancient of Days, 136
Anesthesia, 17
Anger, 17, 36, 54, 60, 67, 72,
  122, 127, 165, 175, 203, 356
  defined, 47

Antahkarana, 15, 70, 238, 263,
  289, 309, 315, 326, 381
  and relations with
    Permanent Atoms, 315
  as the Path, 238
  foundation of, 309
  higher, 15, 381
Anxiety, 17, 57, 95, 117, 129,
  133, 139
Arhat(s), 34, 43, 258, 263,
  267, 304, 335, 387
  defined, 397
Arhathood
  how accomplished, 387
  three processes to, 335
Arjuna, 293, 295
Aryan Race, 90
Ashramic energy
  and unfoldment of petals,
    262
Ashramic group(s)
  admittance into, 390
  and petals and balance, 391
Ashramic group Chalice
  how developed, 389
Aspiration
  and mantrams, 141
Aspirations, 61
Assimilation mechanism
  and levels of mind, 202
Astral body, 34, 89, 166, 197,
  202, 314, 337, 340,
  350-351, 382, 398
  how devastated, 33
  how purified, 372
  maturity of, 261
  passing beyond, 279
Astral body and centers
  and Hall of Learning, 382

409

D

H

Hearing
and observation, 134
Heart, Galactic
and sensitivity to, 364
Heart, unhealthy
causes of , 251
Herd-like behavior
and push-buttons, 21
Hero images
and subc. mind, 195
Hesitation
causes for, 61
Higher Worlds, 8, 91,
140-141, 248, 266-267, 271,
289, 310, 360-361, 367
home in, 367
Hilarity, 18
Hindrances
kinds and effects of, 81
Hitler, 26, 203
Holy Grail, 232-233
Hope, 7, 95, 98, 133, 180, 202
Horror, 17
Human mechanism
value of, 257
Humanitarian(s)
and sacrifice petals, 256
Humanity, spheres of
and contact with, 262
Humiliating others
causes of, 185
Humiliation
kinds of, 183
Hypnotic states
listed, 53
Hypnotic suggestions, 8, 28,
72, 75, 85, 103, 105, 121,
138, 147, 149, 153, 162,
176, 185, 195, 213

Hypnotism, 17, 54-55, 107-108
how to prevent, 116
Hypnotized state
and crises, 122
Hypocricy, 54, 96

I

Ida, 358
Ideas, basic
listed to stand on, 188
Identification, 116
Illness
and effects of, 53
and fear, 125
and nervous system, 340
and subc. mind, 84
Illness, personality
and exercise for, 216
Illness, physical
and effect of hindrances, 81
and subc. mind, 85
Illumination, 73, 252, 257
defined, 67
real, 78
Illusion, 34, 191, 255-256,
261, 306, 327-328, 346, 372
how conquered, 388
origin of, 96
Illusions
defined, 255
Image, of self
and humiliation, 185
Image, positive
building of, 132
Image, ugly
how to clean, 113

M

Q

About the Author

This is Torkom Saraydarian's latest published book. Many more will be released very soon. His vocal and instrumental compositions number in the hundreds and are being released.

The author's books have been used all over the world as sources of guidance and inspiration for true New Age living based on the teachings of the Ageless Wisdom. Some of the books have been translated into other languages, including German, Dutch, Danish, Portuguese, French, Spanish, Italian, Greek, Yugoslavian, and Swedish. He holds lectures and seminars in the United States as well as in other parts of the world.

Torkom Saraydarian's entire life has been a zealous effort to help people live healthy, joyous, and successful lives. He has spread this message of love and true vision tirelessly throughout his life.

From early boyhood the author learned first-hand from teachers of the Ageless Wisdom. He has studied widely in world religions and philosophies. He is in addition an accomplished pianist, violinist, and cellist and plays many other instruments as well. His books, lectures, seminars, and music are inspiring and offer a true insight into the beauty of the Ageless Wisdom.

Torkom Saraydarian's books and music speak to the hearts and minds of a humanity eager for positive change. His books, covering a large spectrum of human existence, are written in straightforward, unpretentious, clear, and often humorous fashion. His works draw on personal experiences, varied and rich. He offers insight and explanations to anyone interested in applying spiritual guidelines to everyday life. His no-nonense approach is practical, simple, and readily accessible to anyone who is interested in finding real meaning in life.

Torkom Saraydarian has de-mystified the mysteries of the Ageless Wisdom. He has made the much needed link between the spiritual and the everyday worlds.

Look for exciting new books, music, and videos being released by Torkom Saraydarian.

Other Books by Torkom Saraydarian

The Ageless Wisdom
The Bhagavad Gita
Breakthrough to Higher Psychism
Challenge For Discipleship
Christ, The Avatar of Sacrificial Love
A Commentary on Psychic Energy
Cosmic Shocks
Cosmos in Man
Dialogue With Christ
Dynamics of Success
Flame of Beauty, Culture, Love, Joy
The Flame of the Heart
Hiawatha and the Great Peace
The Hidden Glory of the Inner Man
I Was
Joy and Healing
Legend of Shamballa
New Dimensions in Healing
Olympus World Report...The Year 3000
Other Worlds
The Psyche and Psychism
The Psychology of Cooperation and Group
    Consciousness
The Purpose of Life
The Science of Becoming Oneself
The Science of Meditation
The Sense of Responsibility in Society
Sex, Family, and the Woman in Society
The Solar Angel

Spiritual Regeneration
Symphony of the Zodiac
Talks on Agni
Triangles of Fire
Unusual Court
Woman, Torch of the Future
The Year 2000 & After

Booklets

A Daily Discipline of Worship
Building Family Unity
Earthquakes and Disasters — What the Ageless
  Wisdom Tells Us
Fiery Carriage and Drugs
Five Great Mantrams of the New Age
Hierarchy and the Plan
Irritation — The Destructive Fire
The Psychology of Cooperation
Questioning Traveler and Karma
Responsibility
The Responsibility of Fathers
The Responsibility of Mothers
Spring of Prosperity
Synthesis
Torchbearers
What to Look for in the Heart of Your Partner

Video

The Seven Rays Interpreted

Next Book Release: **Thought and the Glory of Thinking**

Ordering Information

Write to the publisher for additional information regarding:

— Free catalog of author's books and music tapes

— Lecture tapes and videos

— Placement on mailing list

— New releases

Additional copies of *The Subconscious Mind and the Chalice*

U.S. $18.00
Postage within U.S.A. $3.50
Plus applicable state sales tax

T.S.G. Publishing Foundation, Inc.
Visions for the Twenty-First Century®
P.O. Box 4273
West Hills, California 91308
United States of America

TEL: (818) 888-7850
FAX: (818) 346-6457

T.S.G. Publishing Foundation, Inc. is a non-profit, tax-exempt organization.

Our purpose is to strive to be a pathway for the transformation of humanity. We provide effective tools, by means of the applied Teaching, so that individuals may have the opportunity to transform themselves.

These fine books have been published by the generous donations of the students of the Ageless Wisdom.

Your tax deductible contributions will help us continue publishing and growing.

Our gratitude to all.